WHAT ABOUT TEA?

The whens, whys, and wherefores
of tea,
including 57 recipes

by Donna Forsman

CONTENTS

INTRODUCTION: CONFESSIONS OF A TEA-WINO

I used to have a secret streak of envy for wine snobs. I didn't *like* them, mind you, with their posturing and know-it-all airs. But I envied the obvious joy they derived from an especially fine vintage, the "discoveries" they would make in this or that obscure wine cellar. As a non-drinker, I assumed I was forever locked out of that romantic world of "nose," "bouquet," and "body."

Then I was introduced to the world of fine teas — as different from supermarket teabags as the great French vintages are from a jug of red.

Analogies between wine and tea are very appropriate. They're both natural food products from the earth, subject to infinite variation due to the climate and soil they are grown in, and because of the way they are processed after harvesting. Some teas are even fermented, although in a quite different way from wine.

The terms used by tea tasters will sound familiar to anyone acquainted with wine-tasting. As with wines, the fragrance or "nose" is equally important in fine teas. So is the color of the brewed tea, or infusion, called the "liquor." Teas, like wine, are described as being light or full-bodied. There is even one tea, Oolong, which is referred to as the "champagne" of tea.

TEA DRINKING IN AMERICA

As recently as four or five years ago tea seemed to have reached a nadir of mediocrity in America. Your choice of teas practically boiled down to tea bags or instant. Then the tiny market for fine teas got a boost from an unexpected quarter. Shops specializing in "gourmet" coffees began to spring up everywhere. Following on the heels of the growing popularity of gourmet wines, they offered a comparable selection of fine coffees. And, oh yes, over in the corner, a selection of "gourmet" teas. Tea is a simple way for retailers to add variety to their offerings. Compared to coffee, it is far less perishable and takes up a lot less space.

Now, not content with being a stepsister of gourmet coffee, fine teas are developing a larger-than-ever following of their own. Once you've experimented with different wines and different coffees, why not experiment with different teas as well? Besides, the price of coffee has been escalating faster than gasoline did during the oil embargo.

The trend toward tea drinking is most noticeable in today's young people. Rather than signaling their adulthood by automatically becoming coffee drinkers, many today have adopted tea or herb teas instead. Some consider it healthier; perhaps others are just reflecting a desire to be different. Whatever their reasons, the growing interest in tea will benefit us all, because the more of us tea drinkers there are, the more the marketplace will cater to our demands for the new, the different, and the best.

CHEAP THRILLS

Next to water, tea is the least expensive beverage.

There's no less costly or more pleasurable way to indulge a taste for the best. Even the rarest, finest teas usually cost less than a nickel a cup to prepare.

The range of flavor pleasures available is limited only by imagination. Within the major categories of black, green, and Oolong teas there are numerous flavor differences produced by the specific climate and soil conditions where the teas are grown. From combinations of these teas, countless blends can be made. The addition of herbs, spices, flowers, and fruits produces endless variations of fragrance and taste. There is truly a tea for every taste. For every mood. For every occasion.

Even without the crutch of "bags" or "instant," tea is a simple pleasure to enjoy at home, on the road, or even on the remotest backpacking excursion into the wilderness. Unlike coffee, which loses its flavor quickly after roasting and grinding, tea keeps extremely well. Store it dry and away from extremes of heat or light, and it will retain its full flavor for over a year.

THE START OF A LIFELONG ADVENTURE

The story of tea is as fascinating as the endlessly varying brew itself. This book is intended to be an introduction to that story. The complete tale could fill a library. Hopefully, this taste of tea knowledge will inspire you to explore tea's wealth of taste experiences. Perhaps tea will never be more for you than a sometimes-drink or a change of pace. But if, like me, you adopt tea for good, you'll have found a loyal friend to cheer you out of the blues and get you going when your body says "stay put."

Thank God for tea! What would the world do without tea? . . . how did it exist? I am glad I was not born before tea.

Sydney Smith, 1771–1845

Bitter t'u is called ch'a, hsuan, and yu. It grows in winter in the valleys by the streams and on the hills of Ichow, and does not perish in severe winter. It is gathered on the third day of the third month and then dried. It is good for tumors or abscesses that come about the head, or for ailments of the bladder. It dissipates heat caused by phlegms, or inflammation of the chest. It quenches thirst. It lessens the desire for sleep. It gladdens and cheers the heart.

Emperor Shen Nung, *Pen t'sao*

THE HISTORY OF TEA: FROM MYTH TO POLITICS

Tea is as old as legend. The description above, first transcribed in the second or third century A.D., was supposedly written in 2737 B.C. by the legendary Emperor Shen Nung, the Divine Cultivator or Divine Healer. Legend credits Shen Nung with having "discovered" tea when some leaves from a nearby bush dropped into the water he was boiling.

A Japanese legend credits the discovery of tea to the Indian saint Bodhidharma (Daruma), the founder of Japanese Zen Buddhism. Daruma supposedly travelled to China in 520 A.D., where the Emperor Liang Wu Ti gave him a temple-cave near his capital in Nanking. Here Daruma sat in sleepless meditation for nine years. One day he grew drowsy. In anger at his weakness, he cut off his eyelids. Where drops of his blood touched the ground, a holy plant appeared which made a drink that lessened the desire for sleep.

Although the specifics of the tale make it clearly myth rather than history, the Indian association is significant. Tea is found growing wild only where Longitude 100 East crosses the Tropic of Cancer (the border region of India, Burma, China, and Tibet). It is not at all far-fetched that tea could have been introduced to China by the holy men who travelled between these countries. It is also interesting that while tea grows wild in India, it did not begin to be cultivated there until the nineteenth century, when the British lost their China tea monopoly.

One difficulty with crediting any written reference to tea before the seventh century is that the same Chinese character was used for both tea and another herb, the sow thistle. Another difficulty was the custom of each Dynasty, when gaining power, to rewrite the history of China to reflect the prevailing philosophy of the time. To give their views deeper roots in history, an earlier date might be attributed to a particular event.

By the T'ang Dynasty, the character for tea ("木") was clearly differentiated. In 780 A.D., the publication of the *Ch'a Ching*, or *Tea Classic*, established the undisputed status of tea not only as a commodity, but as an important aspect of Chinese culture. Written by the poet-scholar Lu Yu at the request of merchants interested in promoting the tea trade, this three-volume classic describes in enormous detail the history and varieties of tea, the utensils and method for its preparation, and a glowing description of tea's virtues. Written at a time when all the arts were flowering under the influence of one of China's most cosmopolitan dynasties, the *Ch'a Ching* elevated tea drinking to an art, and made Lu Yu so famous he eventually came to be considered the patron saint of tea merchants.

Tea at this time was compressed into cakes that were easily transported, and gained in value the farther they were carried from where the tea was grown. The currency of the time, on the other hand, diminished in value the farther it moved away from the seat of power where it was issued. Tea was literally more valuable than money.

To prepare this cake (or brick) tea, it was roasted, then shredded and boiled with flavorings such as salt, garlic, orange peel, and onion.

A tea tax levied in 793 A.D. is an indication of how important tea had become as an item of trade. One object of this trade was the Tartars, who appeared along the northern borders of China during the Sui and T'ang Dynasties.

Overland camel-back tea caravans eventually stretched all the way to Moscow. In 1735, Russia's Empress Elizabeth established a regular caravan trade with China. In exchange for tea, the Russians offered furs, a commodity valued by the ruling northern Manchus.

As many as 300 camels, each loaded with about 600 pounds of brick tea, would make up a caravan. The 11,000-mile route from Peking to Moscow spanned deserts and mountains. The average caravan took sixteen months to reach its destination. When the Trans-Siberian Railway was completed in 1900, travel time was cut to a mere seven weeks, and the romantic camel caravans disappeared.

When the Mongols overran northern China and established the Yuan Dynasty (1260–1368), they overlooked tea, whose production was centered in the south. This probably explains why there is no mention of tea in Marco Polo's description of his visit to the Imperial Court of Kubla Khan. It wasn't until the Ming Dynasty, and the revival of the traditional arts, that Westerners first met tea in China.

TEA IN JAPAN

Tea travelled to Japan along with the monks who introduced Buddhism to the Japanese. In 727 A.D., the Emperor Shomu served tea to a hundred monks at his palace in Nara. In 794 A.D., the Emperor Kammu planted tea in his Imperial Gardens and established a special government position, the Supervisor of the Tea Gardens.

Tea drinking had become a well-established part of Ch'an, the Zen Buddhist ceremony in both China and Japan. Since Buddhism and Taoism were the religions of the masses, tea became the drink of the common people.

The form of tea used during the Sung Dynasty was the form transported to Japan. Dried green tea leaves were ground into a fine powder, then whipped to a froth in boiling water using a bamboo whisk. This form of tea survives to this day as a part of the Japanese Tea Ceremony.

The first significant Japanese work on tea was the *Book of Tea Sanitation*, written in 1191 A.D. by Yeisai, who had travelled to China to study Zen Buddhism. His book was undoubtedly modeled on Lu Yu's *Tea Classic*. But by the fifteenth century, Japanese tea culture had developed its own very difinite characteristics. The Cha-no-yu ("hot-water tea") ceremony had been refined into a highly stylized ritual. Yoshimasa, the Ashikaga shogun, added a tea chamber to his palace, and made the Buddhist priest Shoko the first high priest of Cha-no-yu.

In 1584, Sen-no Rikyu built the first independent Japanese tea house, and formulated the "Rules for the Tea Ceremony," which have remained largely unchanged to this day. James Mitchener gives a detailed account of this ceremony and other aspects of Japanese Samuraix culture in his novel *Shogun,* which dramatizes the early dealings between Europeans and the Japanese.

EUROPE ACQUIRES A TASTE FOR TEA

Until the end of the fifteenth century, European trade with the East was limited to overland routes controlled by the Arabs. Venice was the center for this trade, with the Dutch supplying gold and European merchandise to exchange for the silks and spices brought by the Arabs from India and China. The Venetian author, Giambattista Ramusio, wrote in 1559 what may be the first European reference to tea. His report is based on a story told him by the Persian merchant Hajji Mahommed:

> He told me that all over Cathay they made use of another plant or rather of its leaves. This is called by those people *Chai Catai,* and grows in the district of Cathay which is called Cacian-fu. This is commonly used and much esteemed over all those countries. They take of that herb, whether dry or fresh, and boil it well in water. One or two cups of this decoction taken on an empty stomach removes fever, headache, stomach ache, pain in the side or in the joints, and it should be taken as hot as you can bear it. He said, besides, that it was good for no end of other ailments which he could not remember, but gout was one of them. And if it happens that one feels incommoded in the stomach for having eaten too much, one has but to take a little of this decoction, and in a short time all will be digested. And it is so highly valued and esteemed that every one going on a journey takes it with him, and those people would gladly give a sack of rhubarb[1] for one ounce of *Chai catai.*

By the sixteenth century, the Spanish and Portuguese had developed long-range sailing fleets, and were no longer content to leave the lucrative Eastern trade in Arab hands. By 1557, the Portuguese had established a trading port on the Chinese island of Macao, the beginning of a Portuguese monopoly of the China trade. The European end of this trading route was handled by the Dutch, who controlled European banking and trade of precious metals. The Chinese were conspicuously uninterested in European products. Silver was virtually the only foreign substance they would accept in trade.[2]

---

1. Rhubarb was used medicinally by the Chinese as an aid to digestion. Imported Chinese rhubarb was sought-after by the heavy-eating Europeans. At one point, a Chinese official, anxious to be rid of the bothersome British, suggested halting the rhubarb trade, which would leave the "ocean devils" incapacitated with belly aches.

2. The British later discovered another, opium, which was grown in

Since the profit of the China trade was so apparent to the Dutch, it was only logical that they would seek a larger share. By the end of the sixteenth century, Holland had broken away from Spain to become an independent republic. Her power as a seagoing nation was growing. Four Dutch ships that reached the East Indies established a trading depot at Bantam, Java.

By 1600, the Dutch had 10,000 ships at sea, a ruinously competitive situation. The solution was to form the East India Company, a monopoly that could control the volume of trade to maintain a high level of profit for all. The Company was granted such broad powers by *The Lords Seventeen,* a governing council comprised of merchants from each province, that it virtually functioned as a government in the East, waging war against the Spanish and Portuguese.

The Dutch had begun buying tea from the Portuguese on Macao in 1606, but they soon sailed to Japan, where they gained Japanese favor by helping dislodge the hated Portuguese, who had entrenched themselves in a walled settlement overlooking Nagasaki harbor. In return for unseating the Portuguese, the Japanese gave the Dutch permission to trade for Japanese tea from an island in Nagasaki harbor.

But just as the Portuguese could not hold a monopoly on this lucrative trade, neither could the Dutch. Tea, which reached England by way of Holland, was selling in London for the equivalent of $30 to $50 a pound. With the defeat of the Spanish Armada, Britain had established herself as a mighty seagoing power. In 1600, the British East India Company was chartered with the power to establish by-laws, to export goods and foreign coin or bullion duty-free, and to impose fines and mete out punishments. By 1630, the company had established trading factories in India. In 1637, four British ships forced their way past the Portuguese at Macao and sailed up the Canton River. They established a factory at Amoy in Fukien province. It is from the Fukien word "t'e" that our English word "tea" evolved.

By the mid-seventeenth century, the Dutch had also been granted trade concessions through Canton. Since Manchu law prohibited nobility from engaging in com-

India and traded illegally for China tea and silver. Opium use became not only a menace to Chinese health and well being, but also a burden on the economy. Eventually the illegal traffic led to the ill-fated Opium Wars, which opened China to still further Western exploitation.

merce, trade was negotiated through the "hoppo," a lower-class official who maintained his position through bribes to his patron at court.

By this time tea had evolved from the frothy whipped beverage that survives in Japan to the familiar steeped leaves we know in the West. This is the form of tea that took Europe by storm.

TEA, THE FASHIONABLE DRINK

Tea was first sold in Holland by apothecaries. It was sold by the ounce along with other costly Eastern spices, but its popularity was enormous nonetheless. Some families are said to have bankrupted themselves giving elaborate tea parties.

In London, tea became a featured drink at coffee houses. In a diary entry dated September 20, 1660, Samuel Pepys mentions trying tea at his coffee house. That same year, Charles II levied a tax on tea because its popularity had caused such a decline in liquor revenues. Charles' wife, Catherine of Braganza, was the first tea-drinking English Queen. She brought the custom with her from her native Portugal, and may have been influential in its popularization in England.

In 1667, a law was passed forbidding the importation of tea from Holland. This gave the British East India Company a monopoly on Far Eastern goods. Two years later, the first shipment of British East India Company tea reached England. Within ten years, a regular direct trade with China was flourishing.

Tea wasn't received with equal enthusiasm in all parts of Europe. Initial German reaction was favorable, but the Germans soon returned to their preferred brew, beer. In France, a coalition of physicians and patriots denounced tea and mounted a campaign to promote the use of locally grown herbs instead. These "tissanes," which had formerly been used strictly as medicine, became the herb teas the French favor to this day.

In England, tea drinking still centered around coffee houses which remained the province of men. Thomas Twining changed all that. In 1706, next door to his London coffee house, he opened The Golden Lion, the first tea shop. Here women were welcome to sip and to buy. The idea made Twining a rich man and stamped his name permanently on tea history.

TEA AND THE AMERICAN REVOLUTION

Tea was an important commodity to Colonists in America. In some New England colonies, for example, frugal housewives stretched their tea as far as possible, even spreading the spent leaves on buttered bread.

Trouble began brewing in the Colonies when George III imposed the Stamp Act of 1765, which levied a tax on numerous goods (including tea) in order to finance a war between England and France. The American Colonists protested the tax because it had not been approved by their local legislatures. In response to pressure, the Townsend Act was passed in 1767, which removed the tax from all Colonial imports except tea, paper, lead, and paint. The American boycott that resulted was so effective it threatened to bankrupt the British East India Company. All the duties were repealed except the duty on tea, which was kept largely as a symbol of the Parliament's power to tax the colonies. In addition, the British East India Company was granted a monopoly to export tea directly to America, cutting American merchants out of the picture. Tea boycotts solidified in the face of this favoritism. Committees of Correspondence were organized to coordinate resistance among the Colonies.

On November 28, 1773, a group of patriots, dressed and painted to look like Indians, boarded three ships in Boston harbor. In three hours, they smashed 342 chests of tea, dumping the contents into the harbor. Word of the "Boston Tea Party" quickly spread to the other Colonies, where similar tea parties were staged. Parliament retaliated by closing the port of Boston. The Boston charter was revised so that the town council was appointed rather than elected. As one repressive act followed the next, revolution was inevitable, and tea drinking came to be considered as unpatriotic as flying the Union Jack.

SMUGGLED TEA AND PSEUDO-TEA

The same high tea duties that helped precipitate the American Revolution also had a powerful impact in England. Rather than fomenting revolution, they pro-

moted highly organized smuggling and rampant adulteration of tea. Around this time it was estimated that two-thirds of the tea drunk in England was being smuggled in. Most of this tea came from Holland by way of small Dutch ships that anchored in the fog off Cornwall, Dorset, and Kent. Under cover of night the tea was transferred to English fishing boats, which took it to caves and even church crypts along the coast. Pony caravans completed the last leg of the journey to the retailers. The business was so lucrative it lured many a fisherman and farmer away from their traditional occupations. The threat to the economy forced Prime Minister William Pitt to repeal the tea duties in 1784.

THE CHINA CLIPPERS

In 1834, the British East India Company's monopoly in the China trade expired. At about the same time in America, a swift new sailing vessel that had evolved from the privateers of the War of 1812, was put on the China run. This was the forerunner of the tea clipper, a sleek new type of ship capable of incredible speeds.

The first real tea clipper, the *Rainbow,* was launched in New York in 1845. Her maiden voyage earned her owners the cost of her construction plus an equal amount of profit. Her second voyage brought her home in less time than conventional ships took just to get to Canton so she was the first ship to bring back news that she had arrived in China! The race was on.

The first British tea clipper was built in 1850. Fortunately for the British, American competition in the China trade had been diverted by the need for speedy ships to carry would-be miners to the gold fields in California. But competition among Britons themselves was fierce. In the decade beginning in 1860, 26 tea clippers were built, including the *Cutty Sark, Ariel, Thermopylae,* and *Taeping.* Each year these ships raced to be the first to England with the new crop of tea.

The opening of the Suez Canal was the beginning of the end of this glamorous era. Most of the tea clippers eventually retired to the Australian wool run, with steamships inheriting the honor of bringing the world its cup of tea.

TEA MOVES WEST

Tea grows wild in parts of India, but the British didn't notice (or didn't *choose* to notice) as long as they had the lucrative China monopoly. It is probably no coincidence that serious and systematic efforts towards tea cultivation in India began in 1834, one year after the British East India Company's China monopoly expired. The earliest attempts involved importing Chinese tea seeds, plants, and even labor. But eventually the native tea plants of Assam were successfully domesticated. Cultivation, which started in Assam, soon spread to Darjeeling, Cachar, Sylhet, and other regions.

The Dutch had attempted tea cultivation in Java as early as 1684, but it was in the nineteenth century that their efforts there and in Sumatra began to pay off.

Starting in the 1820s, Ceylon had developed a thriving coffee industry. In 1869, a blight appeared that wiped out the coffee industry in ten years time. By 1875, a thousand acres of tea had been planted. Within twenty years, it had mushroomed to 300,000 acres, and Ceylon was becoming the world's largest supplier of tea.

The British brought tea cultivation to Africa in the beginning of the twentieth century. Plantations established in Colonial Nyasaland, Kenya, and Uganda have continued to thrive under independent rule in these countries.

As early as 1775 tea cultivation was attempted in America. Andre Michaux, a French botanist, experimented with tea near Charleston, South Carolina. During the nineteenth century, a number of experiments were made in several parts of the South, but none proved particularly successful. In this hemisphere, tea has become an important commercial crop only in South America.

TEACUP FORTUNES

"All the tea in China" is an apt way to describe something so vast, so valuable, as to defy the imagination, and the value of China's tea captured the imagination of many a laissez-faire capitalist and contributed to several well-known fortunes.

John Jacob Astor was a German butcher's son. He emigrated first to England, where he worked in his brothers' music shop until he saved enough money for passage to America. Aboard ship he learned of the lucrative American fur trade. Once in New York, he took a job beating moths out of furs — doing anything to learn the business. With his savings he opened his own shop, selling furs as well as pianos he imported from his brothers' European firm. Although Astor's fortune was made in furs and pianos, it was considerably expanded when he initiated a scheme to ship American furs to China, where they were traded for tea. The tea was then shipped to America to be sold at a great profit.

One of our largest supermarket chains, A & P, or "The Great Atlantic & Pacific Tea Company," started out as a mail-order business selling tea, coffee, and spices. One of the founders, George F. Gilman, was so eccentric that even after the business had become a multi-million dollar chain, he insisted that the first dollar taken in each day by every store be mailed directly to him.

Another immigrant, who had perhaps the greatest impact on American tea marketing, was Thomas J. Lipton. A Scotsman, Lipton made enough money in America to return to Glasgow and open a small provisions shop. Lipton had a born gift for promotion. He staged a parade of formally dressed pigs called "Lipton's Orphans" that made his shop famous. With the profits from his shop, Lipton purchased a tea estate in Ceylon. Eventually he opened a wholesale tea business in America. The teas that now carry his name are by far the largest selling brand in the United States, as well as being sold worldwide.

NEW DIRECTIONS

The two best-known, if dubious, American contributions to the history of tea are iced tea . . . and the teabag. The invention of iced tea is credited to Richard Blechynden, an Englishman who was promoting Indian and Ceylonese tea at the 1904 St. Louis World's Fair when a heat-wave threatened to dissolve his business. He added ice, offered it as a cooler, and established an American standby.

The tea bag, on the other hand, wasn't so much invented as discovered. In 1908, Thomas Sullivan, a New York tea importer, mailed his customers some tea samples packaged in small silk bags. He started getting requests, not for the teas, but for the bags, which people assumed were for steeping the tea. The tea bag was born.

Instant tea was something that different people had been playing around with for years. But it never caught on until a product that dissolved in cold water was developed in 1956. Now, instant tea, plain or with additives like sugar and lemon, is one of the fastest growing areas of tea marketing. Unfortunately, convenience is more important to a lot of people than flavor.

At a recent Canton Trade Fair, the Chinese showed samples of freeze-dried tea. It will be interesting to see whether the inventors of the world's oldest forms of tea can successfully promote the world's newest form.

CULTIVATION: FROM BUSH TO BREW

Tea, wherever it is grown, whatever its flavor or color, is all from the same plant, the *Camellia Sinensis*. This hardy evergreen shrub is part of the same family as our flowering garden camellia. The plants even look very similar, with their glossy dark green leaves. In cultivation, the tea bush is kept pruned to a height of three or four feet for convenient plucking, but wild, or left untrimmed, it grows into a tree as tall as thirty feet.

Tea's natural habitat is the monsoon-swept mountain forests of the area where China, India, Tibet, and Burma meet. It grows best in areas where the soil and climate resemble this natural habitat, but tea is grown in acid soils of a variety of textures, from sea level up to 7,000 feet. The best teas are often those that are "high grown," at elevations over 3,000 feet. In some places, certain types of trees are interspersed with the tea bushes to provide nutrients and partial shade for the tea leaves. These teas are sometimes designated as shade grown.

The part of *Camellia Sinensis* used to make tea is the fresh young leaves, known as "flush." For the better grades of tea, only the bud and first two leaves are plucked. The presence of stems and older, tougher leaves in tea is an indication of inferior tea.

The flush is plucked by hand, most often by nimble-fingered women who can pick sixty to eighty pounds in a day. There are usually several harvests a year. The flavor, body, and other qualities can vary enormously from one plucking to another. In most regions, the first (spring) flush is considered the best. But this isn't always so. It depends on the pattern of rainfall, temperature, and other changeable factors. Only if you have detailed knowledge of the region where the tea is grown will information about the particular plucking be meaningful.

Once the flush is plucked, it may be processed in a variety of ways to produce the different sorts of tea that ultimately reach your teapot. The three major processes produce green (unfermented), black (fermented), or Oolong (semi-fermented) tea. A fourth form, called "white tea," is produced only in China and has yet to make its appearance in the United States.

BLACK TEA

Almost all the tea consumed today in America is black tea. Blacks are considered the red wines of tea. The black color results from fermentation, or oxidation, during the processing of the leaves.

The first step in processing black tea is to spread the leaves on racks to wither for up to twenty-four hours. This makes the leaves more pliable and reduces the moisture content.

The withered leaves are then rolled to release their flavorful juices and enzymes. During rolling, the tea takes on the characteristic shape or twist you see in loose tea. Leaves that stick together in the rolling are separated by roll-breakers (vibrating sieves).

Fermentation, which has begun in the rolling machines, continues as the leaves are spread out on a smooth floor or rack. Slowly the leaves begin to turn the color of a new copper penny. The length of fermentation is determined by the flavor characteristics the tea producer chooses to develop. The more the tannin in the leaves oxidizes, the less pungent it becomes. At the same time, the infused liquor will become thicker and redder the longer the leaves are fermented.

Fermentation is halted by firing the tea with blasts of dry hot air. The temperature and finished moisture content must be precisely controlled to produce a tea with good keeping and brewing qualities.

The dried leaves are next sorted by sifting them through a series of progressively finer sieves. This produces the different sizes, called "grades," of black tea: Flowery Orange Pekoe, Orange Pekoe, Pekoe, Souchong, Broken Orange Pekoe, etc., down to the smallest sizes called Fannings and Dust. The use of these "grades" in advertising by major tea packagers has probably produced nothing but confusion among the public. No one grade is "best." Knowing that a particular black tea is Orange Pekoe doesn't tell you a thing about how it will taste. The term Orange Pekoe (pronounced peck-o) is from the Chinese. It referred originally to the presence of whitish tips in the tea that resembled orange blossoms. Properly used, it now refers to whole-leaf tea of a particular size and shape. Open up some of the teabags you see marked Orange Pekoe and what you'll probably find is fannings or dust.

Fine black teas come in many sizes and from many different regions. Your best assurance of quality is to buy from a dealer who takes pride in her or his products and chooses only the best teas, regardless of price.

GREEN TEA

At one time, about half of the tea consumed in the world was green tea. Now only about 2 percent of the exported teas are green. Green tea was quite popular in the United States until the Second World War, when sources were cut off. It has only recently started to regain a little popularity but still not on a mass scale.

While green tea can be produced anywhere tea is grown, most of it comes from Japan and China. And most of that produced in Japan is consumed in Japan.

Tea leaves destined to become green tea are steamed as soon as possible after plucking. This softens the leaves for rolling and also deactivates the enzymes that could make the leaves oxidize and blacken. Next, the leaves are rolled into one of the characteristic green tea leaf shapes (Gunpowder, Spiderleg, etc.) and fired until they are crisp. The rolling releases the juices that give green tea its flavor. Firing holds these flavors in the leaf until they are released by brewing.

Not all green teas are green. Some of the Japanese basket-fired teas are grassy green. But some of the fine China Young Hysons and Imperials are quite blue or silvery grey.

Green teas are considered the white wines of tea. The liquor is usually quite pale, and the flavor can be extremely subtle. But the mild-mannered appearance of the brews isn't always an indication of mildness. Green teas can carry a wallop.

Besides being described by their place of origin, green teas are often described by their leaf style and method of firing. These descriptions are helpful in predicting the quality of the tea. (Not so for black teas.) These descriptions are also specific to the tea's country of origin.

OOLONG TEA

Oolong, the "champagne" of tea, is a compromise between green and black teas. The leaves are partially fermented, then fired to halt the fermentation at a stage that produces an amber-liquored brew with some of the characteristics of both black and green teas. Good Oolong is extremely refreshing and dry, yet fruity.

A well-made Oolong should not be overly fermented. The color of the infusion is your best guide. It should be golden or amber, never red or brown.

Pouchong is Oolong tea to which jasmine or other blossoms are added before the final firing. These are also called "scented teas." The presence of blossoms in the finished product is not an indication of quality; it may be just the opposite. In carefully made scented teas, the blossoms are sifted out after the tea has absorbed their flavor and aroma.

SOME TEA-TASTER'S TERMS DEFINED

AGONY OF THE LEAVES: Describes the unfolding of the tea leaves in boiling water.

BITTER: Refers to a property of tannic acid; an undesirable characteristic in tea.

BODY: The mouth-feel or "weight" of the tea, determined by the amount of soluble solids.

BRIGHT: Describes a sparkling liquor.

BRISK: Lively in the mouth, the opposite of flat.

COPPERY: Describes an infusion the color of a new penny.

CREAM DOWN: The tendency of certain teas to produce a milky substance that rises to the surface, accompanied by a thickening of the liquor. Believed to be caused by precipitation of tannin and caffeine. The phenomenon is associated with certain extremely fine teas.

FLAT: Lacking in briskness and pungency.

FULL: Strong without being bitter.

GONE OFF: Moldy or tainted, also called "sweetish."

MALTY: Used to describe high-fired teas.

METALLIC: Coppery in taste.

MUSTY: Mildew-tainted.

NOSE: Aroma.

POINT: An intensity of flavor, a positive highlight.

PUNGENT: Astringent in the mouth.

RASPING: Coarse in flavor.

RAWNESS: Bitter taste.

ROUGHNESS: Harsh taste.

SAPPY: A full-bodied tea.

SELF-DRINKER: A tea that is suitable for drinking without blending.

SOFT: Smooth and gentle.

STANDS UP: The liquor retains its original color over prolonged steeping.

STAND-OUT: A tea that has character and body.

STEWY: Describes a tea that lacks point.

STRENGTH: Thick liquor, pungent and brisk.

SWEET: Refers to a desirable taste highlight.

TARRY: Having a smoky aroma.

THICK: Describes a concentrated, red infusion.

THIN: Lacking color and body even when properly brewed.

WEAK: Having a thin liquor.

THE PROFESSIONAL TEA TASTER

Professional tea tasting is both a talent and a skill. Not everyone's taste buds can distinguish the subtleties between nearly identical teas. Even someone with the born ability must spend years of tasting and memorizing to be able to identify a tea not only by its region, but by its estate, and by the particular plucking it represents. A skilled taster may remember, by taste, well over a thousand teas.

In Sri Lanka (formerly called Ceylon), young boys spend seven years assisting the tasters before they can hope to become tasters themselves. Of course, many of them never make it. Those who do are employed by major packers and importers from around the world to taste on their behalf at the tea auctions.

The flavor of tea leaves, even from the same bush, varies from one season to another, even from one week to the next, because the rainfall may be more or less, the weather hotter or cooler. But a tea packager's customer expects his blend to taste the same and have the same color and fragrance year in and year out, so the

taster may be tasting to find teas to match an established flavor, color, and fragrance. He may reject a tea not because of any inherent negatives, but simply because it doesn't fit his client's needs.

In a white room (preferably with indirect northern light so that color can accurately be compared), the samples are laid out on a long table. Each sample to be tasted is weighed out on the same scale and placed in small white china pot. Next to it is a sample of the dry leaf, which will be inspected for such qualities as color, leaf size and style, and presence or absence of stems. Fresh water is brought to a boil and measured onto the leaves in each china pot. A timer is set to precisely control the steeping time. When the timer rings, the tea is strained into a white china cup. The leaves are displayed in the inverted lid of the pot.

The taster moves quickly down the row, sniffing, tasting, and pushing aside the obvious rejects. The tasting itself is far from genteel. The tea is sucked into the mouth with plenty of air (and noise). It is quickly gargled around the tongue and then spit into a special waist-high spittoon.

This process is repeated until the field is narrowed to a few samples. At this point the taster may choose to add a measured amount of milk to each remaining sample to bring out more subtleties of seemingly identical teas.

The details of professional tea tasting may vary slightly from one country to another. In America the taster may sit at a round, lazy Susan table on which the samples can be rotated to the taster. The light may be artificial rather than natural, but the general principles are the same.

HOW TEA IS SOLD

Tea, like tobacco, is sold at auction. The major auction centers are in the countries that produce the teas, plus in London and Amsterdam.

Before the auction, a hole is bored into each foil-lined tea chest and a sample taken for tasting. After the tastings are completed, the 110-pound chests are quickly auctioned off in lots of thirty to forty chests. It is not unusual for two million pounds of tea to be auctioned in a single day.

WHAT TEA GOES THROUGH TO GET INTO THE U.S.

Few commodities imported into the United States receive the degree of scrutiny to which tea is subjected. Of the precious few really qualified tea tasters in the U.S., three are employees of the Food and Drug Administration. It is their job to make sure that every shipment of imported tea meets the requirements established by the U.S. Board of Tea Experts.

Established by the Tea Importation Act of 1897, the Board of Tea Experts consists of one government representative and six representatives of the American tea industry. Each year they meet and taste samples submitted by all the major packers and importers. From these samples they establish minimum requirements for every major category of tea.

When a shipment of tea arrives in the U.S., it is put in a bonded warehouse until the FDA inspector tastes and examines it. If it does not meet the minimum standards for that type of tea, it is rejected. Rejected tea must be destroyed or shipped back at the importer's expense.

In 1970, Richard Nixon decided to eliminate the Board of Tea Experts as part of an economy drive. The decision was quickly reversed when it was discovered that under the terms of the Tea Importation Act, *no* tea could be imported without the Board's approval. No Board, no tea.

HOW GOOD IS MOST TEA?

The standards established by the U.S. Board of Tea Experts are only as high as industry wants them to be. In recent years, with rising costs of labor, transportation, and packaging, many tea packagers have kept their retail prices down by actually paying less and less for the tea they buy. The packaged tea you buy today is probably a much chaper *quality* tea than it was a decade ago — even though you're paying more for it.

For the small difference in cost per cup, it pays more than ever to patronize a dealer who specializes in fine teas. The best buy for your money is loose tea your dealer buys by the chest and sells to you by the quarter pound, half-pound, or full pound. For one thing, you'll know the money you're spending is for tea, not a fancy package. Also, you'll have the opportunity to ask questions and examine the tea.

One encouraging trend in the marketing of fine teas is shops that sell tea by the cup or pot as well as by the pound. It's the same way Thomas Twining sold tea back in 1706. A great idea whose time has come . . . again. How better to choose a tea than to taste it? You don't have to be a professional to know what you like.

A WORLD OF TEAS

INDIA

India produces nearly a billion pounds of tea a year, virtually all of which is processed as black tea. Half is consumed in India, the rest exported, principally to England and the Commonwealth countries. The tea-growing regions are mostly in the north and northwest, along the edges of the Himalayas. The exceptions are a group of estates near the southernmost tip of India. These southern regions produce teas similar in character to the "Ceylon" teas of neighboring Sri Lanka.

Teas of only two Indian regions are likely to be found unblended: Darjeeling and Assam. Teas from all the other regions are usually blended and labeled simply "Indian."

DARJEELING

Darjeeling is a district in northeastern India, in the foothills of the Himalayas (if you consider foothills to include elevations up to 6,500 feet). The higher-grown Darjeelings are considered the best. The famous "Darjeeling mist" starts enveloping the plantations at about 4,000 feet. The best flushes are the second, harvested in June, and the autumnal, in October. Darjeeling tea has been described as having the flavor of muscat grapes. Its aroma is fine and sweet, the color a rich golden red. The flavor is mild, yet distinctive, never bitter or biting even if over-extracted. The Russians buy all the Darjeeling they can get, which is one of the reasons it costs so much. Personally, I consider a fine Darjeeling well worth the price. But like all teas, there are many grades of Darjeeling. "Darjeeling blends" may contain only a small percentage of the finer grades, if any.

If you prefer a stronger, more "gutsy" brew, another region's leaf may be more your cup of tea.

ASSAM

The teas called Assams are from the Brahmaputra Valley, part of the Assam Valley, the region of India closest to China. The Assams are bold, rich teas, heavy and pungent. The best have a somewhat malty flavor. The medium-quality Assams are sought-after by British tea blenders for their strength and pungency, which balances out more insipid teas in the blend. These are "gutsy" teas, well suited to a coffee drinker's taste.

SRI LANKA (CEYLON)

Sri Lanka (formerly Ceylon) is the island off the southern tip of India. The island produces half a billion pounds of tea a year, most of it for export. All the tea estates of Sri Lanka are now technically owned by the government, although their management is often the same as it was before they were nationalized. Here, as in India, almost all the tea is processed as black tea. The Ceylon teas are judged less by district than by the quality of each particular lot that comes up for auction. Colombo, the capital of Sri Lanka, is one of the world's most important tea auction sites. Agents representing tea importers and packers from all over the world meet here to taste, to judge, and to buy.

The high-grown Ceylons (over 4,000 feet) are considered the best. The choicest flushes are those picked in February and March, and August and September. Ceylons are fully fermented teas, generally softer than the Indian teas. They should brew reddish brown and flavorful.

CHINA

A generation has grown up with China teas as a legend rather than a reality. Fortunately, that is finally beginning to change. China, which exported half the world's tea before World War II, then dropped to a 3 percent share, is again showing interest in promoting her teas abroad. With the removal of America's trade embargos, some of these magnificent teas are finally becoming available here.

Tea in China is usually grown on hilly ground not suited for other more vital crops. Traditionally, tea cultivation was a family affair. The small, irregular plots presented an ill-kempt, rag-tag appearance that prompted a tea expert in 1935 to comment that it was difficult to believe China could produce any good teas, much less so many superb ones. Processing was almost entirely by hand, leaves being rolled between the arches of the feet and clumps being broken up in sacks that children would bash against the ground.

The story today is entirely different. The Cultural Revolution produced a tea revolution as well. Cadres of students were sent to the countryside to work the fields. Government funds were invested to update existing tea plantings and carve out new ones. Machinery was developed to automate practically the entire processing procedure.

A modern Chinese tea plantation is virtually self-sufficient. Yingteh Plantation, 110 miles north of Canton, provides a good example. This 4,600-acre plantation was carved from a wilderness where tigers used to roam. Tea growing and processing are the main activities of the plantation, but all the food for the plantation workers is raised on the plantation as well. A tea machinery factory produces all the machines for Yingteh, using iron and coal from local sources. Yingteh has its own reservoir, which feeds a sophisticated underground irrigation system. The reservoir also supplies the hydroelectric plant that generates the plantation's power.

The plantation manufactures its own organic fertilizer from greens and manure, processed and aged in pits. It is then mixed with water for application through the underground irrigation system. In the fields, broadleaf trees are planted among the tea bushes to shade them from the hot sun and to draw deep moisture up to the tea bushes' roots.

During the growing season, 120,000 pounds of tea leaves are harvested each day and processed in the plantation's factories. The mechanized procedures used are a far cry from the old traditional methods.

What are the results of all this modernization? Some Westerners feared that China's new teas would lose something in the process. But nothing could be further from the truth. Only a few of these teas have become available in the United States, but those few should prove to be just the tip of a most delicious iceberg. Do make a point to taste whatever China teas become available to you. Keep notes. There's little current information to guide you in this area, so become your own expert.

China's teas, rather than being sold at auction, are marketed at semiannual trade fairs in Canton and Kwangchow. The catalogue published by the China National Native Produce and Animal By-Products Import and Export Corporation (maybe the name sounds more appealing in Chinese) gives the best indication of Chinese teas available for export.

China Blacks

The black teas of China were traditionally divided into two large categories, the Northern Congous (pronounced con-gos) and the Southern Congous. The Northern (blackleaf) Congous were considered the burgundies of tea. The Southern (redleaf) Congous were considered the clarets.

The China National Produce Catalogue no longer uses this classification. It divides black teas simply into Congous and Broken Graded Tea. Most are labeled by province name, such as Yunnan. Some are labeled by "type," such as Keemun and Lapsang Souchong. A few, such as Yingteh, are labeled by plantation. The packaged teas also carry brand names such as "Sunflower" and "Sprouting." It would be impossible to describe all of China's teas, black, green, or Oolong. Instead, I have tried to describe the few you are most likely to encounter.

KEEMUN

This is one of the best known and most imitated of China teas. The flavor of English Breakfast blends is supposedly patterned after Keemun tea, but why settle for the imitation when you can now get the real thing? At its best, Keemun is a rich, full tea with an aroma reminiscent of orchids. Look for it. It's worth the search.

YUNNAN

Yunnan, in the southwestern part of China, was not a traditional tea-growing region. Since World War II, it has become a sizeable tea producer. Yunnan teas have stout leaves, making a bright red infusion that is strong and refreshing.

LAPSANG SOUCHONG

Lapsang Souchong is probably one of the most "different" teas. In addition to the usual processing received by black teas, this one is smoked. The result is an aroma and flavor reminiscent of hickory-smoked ham. Some love it dearly. Some won't touch it with a ten-foot pole. In small doses, it adds a distinctive character to black tea blends. The British are especially fond of adding a smidgen to bolster their brew.

PANYONG

Panyong Congous, from Fukien Province, are brisk and pungent, with a bold leaf and a pleasing fragrance.

PINGSUEY

Pingsuey is a region in Chekiang Province better known for its green teas. Pingsuey black tea has the full-bodied liquor associated with an Indian Assam, but at the same time it has the gentleness of a Ceylon.

China Greens

The green teas of China are grown in many regions, the best at higher, mist-enshrouded altitudes. These cool, moist conditions produce tender, flavorful leaves.

China greens are known by a confusing variety of names. Like the blacks, you may see them referred to by province or region names. They are more frequently described by names that refer to their grade or method of manufacture. To compound the confusion, American tea merchants often misuse these names. For instance, I have seen teas labeled "Imperial Gunpowder," when actually, Imperial and Gunpowder are two different grades of similarly shaped teas. Maybe the tea being described was a blend of the two.

GUNPOWDER

No, Gunpowder is not a description of this tea's taste. This is tea made from younger leaves, tightly rolled into tiny balls named for their resemblance to old-fashioned musket shot. The color of the dried leaves is often more gray than green, sometimes even bluish.

PINHEAD

If properly used, this description should apply to the finest grade of Gunpowder tea, whose leaves are rolled into such tiny beads that they resemble pinheads.

IMPERIAL

Imperial is rolled similarly to Gunpowder, but from older, tougher leaves that produce a larger, looser ball.

YOUNG HYSON

This term refers to good China green teas, thinly rolled and twisted.

CHUN MEE

This is the finest grade of Young Hyson. The leaves are small, twisted, and hard.

SOWMEE

Sowmee is also a small, twisted-leaf type of Young Hyson tea.

PAN FIRED

This is a *green* green tea, fired in iron pans over charcoal.

LUNG CHING

Also called *Dragon Well,* this green tea is becoming increasingly popular in the West.

China Oolongs

Almost anything you read about tea will tell you that Mainland China Oolongs are completely inferior to those of Taiwan (Formosa). All this advice seems to be based on the prewar Oolongs of China. The new China Oolongs, grown in Fukien province, show every indication of equaling or bettering those of Taiwan. Taste some and decide for yourself.

Many of these teas have such a fragile fragrance the Chinese drink them after steeping only thirty seconds to a minute. The leaves are then re-infused several times.

TI KUAN YIN

The name means *Iron Goddess of Mercy,* an apt description, because this highly fragrant tea is strong and invigorating. It is made from the choicest leaves, which are big and thick.

WU-I

There are actually a number of Oolong teas from the Wu-I mountains. The best are sweet, fragrant, and delicate.

Scented China Teas

China is deservedly praised for her scented teas. The most famous of these is Jasmine, made with green or Oolong tea. But there are also scented black teas such as Rose and Lychee. The scenting process is a painstaking one. Since the blossoms used aren't usually in bloom at the time the finest grades of tea are plucked, the tea is processed and then stored until the flowers are available.

A controlled quantity of flowers and tea leaves are blended together and tossed gently at a precise temperature over a period of hours until the fragrance and flavor of the flower has been absorbed by the tea leaves. Then the spent flowers are carefully sifted out. This process may be repeated as often as five times to achieve the intensity of scenting desired.

JASMINE

This exotic tea with its heady tropical fragrance may have either a green or Oolong tea base. The scenting is done at night, when the jasmine blossoms open to release their fragrance. This is a pungent, refreshing tea, with an assertive quality.

ROSE

This fragrant black tea will make you feel like you're in a rose garden even when there's snow on the ground. It is distinctly floral, which appeals to many people.

LYCHEE

Sometimes spelled Lichee, this aromatic black tea is a little less overpowering than Rose. Scented with Chinese Lychee, it is a sweet, mellow tea.

TAIWAN (FORMOSA)

Taiwan, an island off Fukien province, is actually a province of China, although under different political control. Formosa, which means "beautiful," is a name given the island by the Portuguese. Taiwan was under Japanese rule for over sixty years. At the end of World War II, the Japanese were forced to return the island to China. In 1949, it became the home of the exiled Chinese Nationalist government.

Tea has been grown on Taiwan since early settlers from tea-growing Fukien arrived hundreds of years ago. Tea production was encouraged under Japanese rule. During the years that Mainland China was absent as an important world tea supplier, Taiwan geared up her production of China-type teas.

FORMOSA OOLONG

This is Taiwan's most famous tea. It has long been considered the world's best Oolong. (See the China section for some dissent on that subject.)

GREEN TEAS

A certain amount of green tea is produced, but most of it goes to North Africa. Taiwan's green teas are labeled Pan-Fired, Gunpowder, etc.

BLACK TEAS

The teas labeled simply "Formosa black" are similar to Assams. They are used in many American blends. Other blacks include Formosa Keemun and Lapsang Souchong.

JASMINE

Taiwan's Jasmine teas are typically made with an Oolong base. The degree of scenting is somewhat less intense than the mainland Jasmines.

JAPAN

Virtually all Japanese tea is green tea. The ritual and care associated with the Japanese Tea Ceremony is also reflected in their approach to raising and processing tea. The most highly prized tea in Japan is Gyokuro, or "Pearl Dew." The gardens are sheltered with special sun screens to provide varying degrees of shade during the growing season. Only the most tender buds are plucked. They are carefully hand rolled, or dried in the open, natural state to make Tencha.

Tencha is sorted by leaf color into Koicha (dark leaf) and Usucha (light leaf). Both are powdered to make Mattcha, the ceremonial tea.

This, of course, is a miniscule fraction of the tea produced in Japan. Most is the ordinary tea called Sencha, of which there are numerous varieties.

PAN-FIRED

These are Senchas fired in metal pans or trays. The curliest of these are known as Guri, similar to China's Young Hyson.

BASKET-FIRED

The finest of the basket-fired teas are called Spider Leg. These are young, supple leaves twisted into long, straight "sticks" as much as two inches long. Well-formed Spider Leg teas are becoming difficult to find. Basket-fired teas have a darker, olive color than pan-fired teas.

NATURAL LEAF

Natural leaf teas may be either pan or basket-fired. The irregular leaf size and shape produces less reliable quality tea. This is sometimes called "porcelain-fired" tea.

BANCHA

Bancha is the poorest grade of Japanese tea. It can include leaf rejected in sorting the better grades, plus the season-end prunings from the tea bushes. Bancha has a certain health food following because of its lower caffeine content. But I have also seen Bancha listed by some merchants as a "gourmet" tea, a practice of questionable ethics.

INDONESIA

Indonesia is the world's fourth largest producer of tea, three-quarters of it from Java, the rest from Sumatra. For all that tea, you've probably never seen a bag or package marked either. Indonesia's teas are good but undistinguished, the staple of many blends.

USSR

Here's another one you'll probably never taste unless you go there. Despite the 130 million pounds a year grown around the eastern end of the Black Sea, Russia still has to import large quantities of tea to satisfy her thirst. The few examples of "Georgian" tea that have shown up in America have been far from gourmet quality. The Russians are obviously keeping the best at home.

The teas you usually see labeled "Russian" are in fact Russian-style blends, their characteristic flavor produced by the inclusion of about 10 percent Lapsang Souchong.

AFRICA

Tea is a relatively new, but increasingly important crop in several East African countries. You won't usually find the teas straight; they are considered blenders. One exception is a Kenyan tea I recently saw listed in a mail order catalogue. I have no idea whether it was actually a fine tea or a promotional gimmick.

SOUTH AMERICA

Coffee isn't the only beverage that grows in South America. Peru, Ecuador, Brazil, and Argentina all grow tea. Argentina's tea exports are increasing steadily. These teas have the advantage to blenders of being inexpensive, fairly innocuous teas. They don't detract from the character of more expensive teas, which can be added in small quantities and still dominate the flavor of the blend.

OTHER AREAS

A limited amount of tea is grown in Turkey, Iran, Thailand, Vietnam, Burma, and Bangladesh. Most of this tea is consumed locally.

TEA BLENDS

Tea blends are well-guarded secrets, and rightly so. A tea packer is more likely to gain fame and fortune from a well-received blend than from a straight tea that any competitor can buy for the right price.

It is impossible to give any accurate taste descriptions for tea blends, even for the most familiar like English Breakfast or Earl Grey. They are "proprietary" items, the taste and formula varying from supplier to supplier. I'll just pass on what scuttlebutt I've heard, and let you find out the rest by tasting around.

EARL GREY

In the early days, tea was custom-blended to a customer's specifications. Thus the original Earl Grey's Blend was the tea blended for the Victorian diplomat, the second Earl Grey. The original formula was given to the Earl by a Mandarin while he was on a diplomatic mission to China. In 1830 he entrusted the formula to an English tea firm, Jackson's of Picadilly, to blend the tea for him. The genuine formula is still Jackson's alone, although they have lost the exclusive use of the name. That doesn't mean there aren't other delicious Earl

Grey's around. One of the best is blended in Copenhagen. (The characteristic scent of Earl Grey's Blend, by the way, is from oil of Bergamot, which is lightly sprayed on the leaves.) One of my favorite teas is *called* Earl Grey, but filled with lavender blossoms. Unorthodox but tasty.

ENGLISH BREAKFAST

Aside from saying that English Breakfast is a blend of black teas, it is difficult to say what it is. The blend was invented for American use — you won't find it in England. It was supposedly patterned after the taste of China Keemun, but don't expect much of a resemblance. In fact, don't expect much of a resemblance from one tea marked English Breakfast to the next.

IRISH BREAKFAST

The Irish blend their tea strong and full-bodied so that it will stand up to the addition of as much as half a cup of milk. If properly blended, you may find this one a bit potent to drink straight.

RUSSIAN STYLE

This blend of black teas may be called by such names as Russian Caravan and Russian Samovar. Such blends often contain about 10 percent Lapsang Souchong, so expect a slightly smoky taste.

SPICED AND HERB BLENDS

These may be blends of green, Oolong, black, or mixed teas, with bits of other ingredients added. They are often also sprayed with oils or flavor extracts for a stronger aroma and flavor of the added "spice." The predominant flavor is usually that of the other ingredients rather than that of the tea. Some purists shun them for this reason. I think that attitude is just as silly as refusing to cook with herbs and spices.

One of the best known spiced teas in this country is *Constant Comment,* made by Bigelow. They're not revealing their secret formula, but obviously orange peel and clove dominate the flavor and aroma.

Ingredients commonly used in spiced teas include cinnamon, cloves, nutmeg, ginger, sassafras, orange, lemon, mint, and chamomile. Try inventing your own spiced tea blends. You've probably got some of the basic ingredients right in your spice rack.

BUYING, STORING AND MAKING TEA

HOW TO SELECT YOUR TEA

Those who attribute smoothness, darkness, and flatness to good tea are connoisseurs of an inferior order; those who attribute wrinkles, yellowness, and uneven surface to good tea are the ordinary connoisseurs; those who hold the opinion that these qualities may or may not belong to good tea are the superior connoisseurs. Because whether tea is good or otherwise depends upon its flavour.

Lu Yu, *Cha Ching* (Tea Classic) 780 A.D.

WHERE TO BUY YOUR TEA

If you're really interested in buying the best teas, at the fairest prices, forget the supermarket. What you're looking for is a store that *specializes* in good teas. Try the yellow pages of the phone book, under "tea," "gourmet shops," or "coffee dealers — retail." If you can't tell from their ad whether they'll have what you want, give them a call.

Ask them if they sell loose tea, as opposed to packaged, branded teas such as Bigelow, Wagners, or Twinings. While these branded teas may be a cut above what the supermarket has to offer, they're rarely as good a *value* as loose teas your dealer buys in bulk and bags for you in quarter, half, or full pounds.

Loose teas give you the opportunity to examine a sample of the leaf before you buy it. This won't tell you anything about how the tea will taste, but it can give you some idea of the tea's freshness. Smell the leaves. Some teas have a pronounced fragrance, some a subtle one. But if you don't smell anything, it is probably a sign of old or improperly stored tea. If the smell is unpleasant, avoid the tea: its aroma is just as important to your taste experience as the flavor is. Squeeze the leaves gently. They should give a little. If they're so brittle they crumble into power, that's another sign the tea may be old.

Teas sell under many different names (some dreamed up by the distributor or the proprietor of the shop). Some shops print up lists describing the taste of their teas. In any case, ask questions. And ask for suggestions. Tell the person who's helping you what you think you like and dislike. It will help her or him make a recommendation that's appropriate for you.

If the store also *serves* tea, by all means do some tasting. Whether you *like* the tea is what it's all about. If they sell sample sizes, indulge yourself. Here's your chance to taste a lot of different teas without breaking the bank. Later you can buy your favorites in the more economical, larger quantities.

LOST IN THE WILDERNESS?

Stores that specialize in fine teas and coffees are popping up in the most unexpected places all over the country. But you may still find yourself out of comfortable traveling distance from any of these oases. Don't despair. There's always mail order. Fortunately, tea travels well. If you order from a reputable firm, you can expect your order to arrive in prime drinking condition. The following is by no means a complete list of mail-order sources, but the ones listed are all well-established businesses that take pride in their teas and their service. Write for their catalogues, then decide for yourself who you'd like to do business with.

EAST INDIA TEA & COFFEE, LTD.
c/o Coffee & Tea, Ltd.
1481 Third Street
San Francisco, CA 94107

East India offers a selection of twenty teas, plus brewing accessories, gift packs, and samplers. All prices include shipping. Regular mailings include an informative newsletter.

GRACE TEA COMPANY, LTD.
799 Broadway
New York, NY 10003

Grace offers a limited selection of nine teas, sold by the half pound and packaged in attractive tins. Also gift assortments. Shipping is 75¢ per half pound, with $1.50 minimum per delivery.

McNULTY'S TEA & COFFEE CO., INC.
109 Christopher Street
New York, NY 10014

McNulty's has been providing New Yorkers with fine teas and coffees for over eighty years. Their mail-order selection includes a huge variety of teas (five different Oolongs). They will also custom-blend to your specifications.

PAPRIKA'S WEISS IMPORTER
1546 Second Avenue
New York, NY 10028

Squeezed into a 64-page catalogue listing everything from Hungarian Paprika to a duck press are listings for fourteen bulk teas, eighteen herb teas, and nine packaged Mainland China teas. Shipping is a flat $2.80, plus an extra dollar if the total order is under $5.

PHILLIPS COFFEE, TEA & SPICES
384 Miller Avenue
Mill Valley, CA 94941

This is the source of the lavender-scented Earl Grey I'm so addicted to. They offer twenty-five teas in all, with a $3 minimum on mail orders. Packaging and handling are a flat-rate 50¢.

SIMPSON & VAIL, INC.
53 Park Place
New York, NY 10007

Simpson & Vail lists twenty-five teas, including three Darjeelings and the only African tea I've ever seen offered as a self-drinker: Kaproret from Kenya. They also list ten herbal teas. The prices seem very reasonable but do not include shipping. The actual total cost is something you won't find out until you're billed.

STARBUCKS COFFEE COMPANY
2000 Western Avenue
Seattle, WA 98121

Don't be put off by the name. *Starbucks* lists twenty-two teas, plus ten herb teas and a page-long list of spices. Shipping charges are lowest to the Northwest, progressively more the farther away you are.

STORING YOUR TEA

Nothing lasts forever, and tea is no exception. But with reasonable storage conditions, tea should keep a good year. Tea can easily absorb moisture and odors. Strong light or heat can also do it in. Keep your tea in a container with a snug lid, away from the garlic and out of the sun, and you shouldn't have any trouble.

Canning jars are good, although they don't keep out the light. The enameled English tins called tea caddies are perfect (if you can find them). They come in quarter, half, and full pound sizes and in a variety of elaborately decorated patterns.

CHOOSING YOUR TEA TOOLS

In different times and places, people have brewed tea in everything from tin cans to jewel-encrusted porcelain. (The Ottoman Emperors imported the finest Chinese porcelain, then had their jewelers enmesh it in silver and gold filigree set with precious stones.)

The "teaspoon" and the "teacup" have become standard items in almost every American household. You probably already have most of what you'd need to brew a proper cup of tea, but if you're shopping, here are some guidelines:

KETTLES: Some metals affect the taste of tea. The kettle or pot in which you boil your tea water ideally should be tin-lined or enameled metal. A kettle with a whistle helps alert you to the moment when the water is the perfect temperature for tea making.

TEAPOTS: Earthenware, china, or glass is best. If you have a silver teapot, by all means use it. But make sure it is tarnish-free and that you've washed out any possible traces of cleaner. A pot that's too big for the amount of tea you are making will quickly rob the tea of its heat.

INFUSERS: An infuser is any of a variety of perforated gadgets used to encase the steeping tea leaves so you don't have to strain them out of your finished brew. Some are on little chains that hang over the lip of the teapot. Some are in the form of spoons, especially handy for making a single cup at a time.

Unfortunately, it is easy to buy the wrong infuser. I've yet to find the perfect one. Most of them are metal. Make sure the one you choose is stainless steel or chrome or silver-plate. One infuser I bought was stainless, but the chain attached to it wasn't and turned an ominous black. If that happens to you, I'd suggest taking it back. The metal is obviously reacting with the tea. Make sure the infuser has plenty of room for the tea you're brewing (you'll learn how to tell in the section called "How to make perfect tea"). Also make sure the water will be able to get to the tea inside. The more holes the better. The best I've seen is a Japanese infuser of very fine stainless steel mesh. Don't buy any infuser without making sure it is easy to open and close. Most take two hands, which can be a nuisance. There's one, an infuser spoon with a spring, that can easily be operated with one hand.

STRAINERS: If you don't use some sort of infuser, you'll probably want to strain your tea. The same advice holds true regarding metals. Look for stainless steel. Some strainers made especially for serving tea come with their own drip stand. These are helpful if you're serving at the table rather than from the kitchen.

COSIES: A tea cosy (or cosie) is an insulated cover for your teapot. You can sometimes find them where fine teas are sold, or you can easily make your own. The homemade versions are often knitted or crocheted. Since the object of a cosy is to keep the tea hot, whatever you make or buy should be thickly padded with a good insulator.

HOW TO MAKE PERFECT TEA

Making good tea needn't involve any complicated ritual. The instructions below only look lengthy because I'm giving you the whys along with the hows. Once you understand the essentials, you'll never need to consult the "recipe" again.

1. *Use the best tea you can buy.* The best tea may seem costly when you see the price per pound. But remember that each pound will give you 160 cups of tea. Calculate the cost per cup. Even the costliest tea is still usually less expensive than coffee or milk or soft drinks.

2. *Start with fresh, pure water.* (Don't use water from the hot water tap. It has lost a lot of its oxygen already. Water that lacks oxygen makes flat tea.) If your local water supply is less than tasty, consider using bottled water or a water-purifying device like the *Watermate*. The investment will benefit not just your tea, but your coffee, drinking water, and cooking as well. In Colonial America certain public water pumps were so highly esteemed for their "tea water" that people came from miles around to cart home a supply. In Europe and New England, famous "tea gardens" grew up around particularly good wells.

3. *Bring the water to a rolling boil.* Don't let the water boil on and on. It will be losing oxygen. But be sure the water *is* boiling. Tea leaves infused at too low a temperature don't open fully to release their fragrant oils.

4. *Measure your tea.* Use one level teaspoon per cup. Put the tea in a clean, prewarmed pot, or a roomy infuser if you're making a single cup. Dried tea leaves are tightly curled. They only release their full flavor when the whole surface of the leaf is exposed to boiling water. Check the leaf after brewing. If parts of it are still stiff or dry, you either didn't steep them long enough, or they were packed together too tightly to get thoroughly soaked.

5. *Steep the recommended time for the tea you are brewing.* When the water has reached a rolling boil, pour it promptly over the tea leaves. Cover and steep three to five minutes for most teas. Whole-leaf teas need longer steeping than broken-leaf teas, green teas longer than black. If you like "weaker" tea, don't skimp on the infusion time. Instead, add extra hot water to the finished brew.

6. *Separate the leaves from the brewed tea.* When the tea has steeped the recommended amount of time, promptly remove the leaves by taking out the infuser or straining the tea. Over-steeping can make even the best tea bitter. If you've made a whole pot of tea, be sure to stir it before pouring so you don't end up with one cup that's too watery, another that's too strong.

7. *Serve and enjoy.* Good quality teas need no other adornment. But if you prefer, feel free to add honey, sugar, milk, or lemon to suit your taste. There are no rules — it's all a matter of what you enjoy.

PERFECT ICED TEA

To compensate for the melting ice, use half again as much tea as you would for hot tea. Keep the brewed tea at room temperature. Refrigeration turns it cloudy. Some teas cloud more easily than others. Add a little hot water to clear the brew.

Here's an easy saucepan method to make two quarts of iced tea at a time:

1. In a stainless steel saucepan, bring one quart of fresh cold water to a rolling boil.

2. Remove from heat and add 1/3 C. loose tea.

3. Stir. Cover and steep five minutes.

4. Stir again. Strain into a pitcher and add one quart cold water.

TEA PARAPHERNALIA

I'm a little teapot, short and stout.
Here is my handle, here is my spout.
When I get all steamed up, then I shout.
Just tip me over and pour me out.

Children's rhyme

The earliest Chinese method that we know for preparing tea was to break off a chunk of the brick of compressed tea leaves and drop it into a kettle of water. This required nothing more than a simple pot or kettle hanging over an open fire.

By the Sung Dynasty, powdered tea had become fashionable. This was whipped with a bamboo whisk in the bowl or cup in which it would be served. Porcelain *Chien* ware cups of dark purple or blackish brown were used by collectors and connoisseurs in tea tasting contests.

In Japan, the development of the tea ceremony produced a whole range of specialized tea implements, from bamboo water dippers, whisks, and tea spoons to kettles and bowls. The style of these implements was strongly influenced by Sen-no Rikyu, who is considered Japan's greatest Tea Master. Rikyu stressed the simple and the humble. His most cherished tea bowls were made by Chojiro, the son of a Korean tile maker. These were soft, earthenware bowls, purposely irregular and wide-bottomed in the Korean style.

The fame of the pottery produced by Chojiro and his family eventually earned his younger brother Jokei a gold seal from the shogun Hideyoshi. Jokei took the name from the seal, *raku*, as the family name. To this day it is the name given this earthy style of pottery.

It wasn't until the Ming Dynasty in China, and the development of steeped tea, that specialized containers were designed for brewing tea. The earliest recorded teapots, dated about 1500 A.D., were from Yi-Hsing, near Shanghai. The region is famous for its fine red clay, which when high-fired makes hard, heat-resistant stoneware.

The earliest teapots were patterned after the spouted Chinese wine pot. In fact, when tea drinking became widespread in China, it largely replaced wine drinking. Teahouses in China are still called winehouses, even though they don't serve wine.

The unglazed Yi-Hsing teapots were made in an enormous variety of fanciful shapes. Each tiny pot was just large enough for tea for one. Although the Chinese invented such elegant forms of ceramics as porcelain, and used them for their brightly patterned tea cups, the humble unglazed stoneware teapot is still favored by Chinese tea tasters. They claim it not only conserves heat the best, but also captures the ephemeral fragrance of delicate teas like Oolong.

EUROPE ADOPTS TEA . . . AND "CHINA"

When tea began to reach Europe in the early seventeenth century, *Yi-Hsing* teapots were also part of the cargo. The Dutch already had a thriving ceramics production at Delft, but their pottery couldn't stand up to the boiling water used to make tea. Their solution was to copy the unglazed *Yi-Hsing* stoneware.

Two Dutch brothers, Philip and John Elers, took this skill with them to England. They eventually settled in Staffordshire, where the clays were best suited for making the *Yi-Hsing* type of pottery. English "Redware" from Staffordshire is still sought-after, for teapots especially.

Not content with the austere simplicity of unglazed stoneware, the potters of Staffordshire began to experiment not only with different shapes, but also with different glazes. Lead glazing produced a rich, marbled pattern. Salt glazing was done by throwing salt into the kiln at the height of firing. The most enduring developments were made by Josiah Wedgwood. His jasper-ware was made by pigmenting the clay itself, then ornamenting it with cameo-like appliques of white clay. A later Wedgwood development, which he called Queen's-ware, had a smooth, cream-colored surface. It soon became the standard of mass production.

As European potters began to unlock the secrets of Chinese porcelain — or at least to evolve suitable substitutes — great centers of "China" production developed at Dresden, Limoges, Worcester, and Staffordshire. "Tea Equipages" were the mainstay of this early production, and are still an important part today.

Before the arrival of tea, the English ate off pewter, or, if they could afford it, silver. Not surprisingly, the first known English teapot was silver. Presented in 1670 to a member of the East India Company, it looks for all the world like a coffee pot. Only its inscription reveals its true identity. Silver teapots were soon being fashioned in an enormous variety of shapes, with sugar bowls, cream pitchers, trays, and other accessories to match. The reign of Queen Anne saw an unmatched development of the silversmith's art, much of it devoted to tea sets. For a while, silver took a back seat to China sets, but silverware flourished again under King George. It was during his reign that the American patriot Paul Revere crafted some of the most beautiful silver teapots ever made. Even today, with silver so incredibly expensive, a silver tea service is likely to head the list in the Bridal Registry.

Tea cups were originally imported from China along with teapots. With or without saucers, these original cups were tiny and handleless. The English copies grew considerably in size and soon sprouted handles. Their eventual inclusion in virtually every household made them a standard of measurement.

Another standard measure is the teaspoon, a tea accessory that had no Chinese predecessor. The teaspoon holds, logically enough, exactly the amount of tea needed to brew one cup.

A tea accessory that has Chinese ancestry even in its name is the tea caddy. The Chinese *catty* is a unit of weight that was traditionally used to measure tea. The Chinese porcelain tea jar was soon modified because of the high cost of tea in Europe (as much as $50 a pound). The locked boxes that evolved were as elaborate as jewel chests, inlaid with precious woods and embellish-

ed with rare metals. Some were actually pieces of furniture. In the dining room of the Decatur House in Washington, D.C. (now a National Trust Museum), there is a handsome hardwood chest with locked compartments for green and black tea. The mistress of the house would keep the keys, unlocking the chest only when it was time for the servants to prepare tea. As tea became more commonplace, the caddy found its way to the kitchen shelf, and became simplified to the enameled tins we find today.

The tea cosy seems to be a fairly recent invention. These padded teapot covers became popular handcraft items in late Victorian England. Ladies' magazines printed patterns for knitted, crocheted, embroidered, and pieced varieties.

Tea infusers, called balls (or "eggs" in Europe) first appeared in the early nineteenth century. Tea infuser spoons didn't show up until this century.

The nineteenth and early twentieth centuries produced an enormous array of patented teapot designs. These "better mouse traps" include everything from a double-spouted pot to one with a gadget that cranks out the infuser at a specified time. Royle's self-pouring teapot had a built-in piston that would dispense a single cup when you pressed down on the lid. A Mrs. Sarah Guppy patented a pot containing a wire basket for boiling eggs.

All these whimsical solutions to nonexistent problems can rightly be called a tempest in a teapot. The most popular teapots today are not much different from their sixteenth century prototypes. Tea drinking is still a simple pleasure, easily enjoyed.

EVERYBODY'S CUP OF TEA

*You have filled my tea with lumps of
sugar, and though I asked most distinctly
for bread and butter, you have
given me cake.*

        Lady Windermere's Fan, Oscar Wilde

Whether they call it tea, t'e, cha or chai, there's probably not a country in the world where you won't find tea. Tea drinking is an integral part of many vastly different cultures.

In England, a "nice cup of rosey" can solve everything from nervous tension to a political deadlock. (It even provides a sophisticated way of insulting a guest, as in the quote from *Lady Windermere's Fan.*) In Morocco, a glass of mint tea is the prelude to any business transaction. In Burma, tea leaves are eaten as a pickled relish. The why, when, and how of serving tea varies from country to country and gives us a glimpse of the heritage and attitudes of the different peoples.

HOW THE ORIENT TAKES ITS TEA

THE CHA-NO-YU

Japan has probably the most elaborate ceremony ever developed around tea. The form of tea used in the Cha-no-yu, or tea ceremony, is *Mattcha,* a finely powdered green tea that is whisked with hot water into a thick froth. This is the way tea was prepared in China during the Sung Dynasty. It was the Zen masters who carried this form of tea to Japan and, through the centuries, elaborated a ritual around its preparation and serving.

Cha-no-yu was intended to produce spiritual enlightenment through contemplation of the meaning of commonplace events and objects. The traditional setting for the ceremony was a plain room, nine feet square. The room was preferably isolated in a walled garden.

The host would meet his guests at the garden gate and escort them to the tea house. The door of the tea house was made purposely low, forcing the guests to enter crouched or stooping. No talk of worldly matters was allowed within the tea house. Flattery was not permitted.

The room and all the utensils for the ceremony were extremely simple: bamboo screens, an alcove with a scroll or flower arrangement, tatami mats on the floor. There was a charcoal brazier for the fire. The tea kettle was iron, with perhaps a few pebbles placed in the bottom to evoke a pattering sound as the water boiled. When the sound of the steam was like wind in the trees, the host would whisk the powdered tea into a thick frothy drink which he would offer to the chief guest in a small earthenware bowl. The honored guest would sip, then pass the bowl in turn to the other guests.

Conversation centered around the elements of the ceremony, the arrangement of the flowers, or the brushstrokes in the scroll. It was considered polite for the chief guest to ask to examine the tea utensils. These would be passed around, with comments on the skill of the craftsmen who made them. The entire ceremony was serene, tranquil. Conversation was in hushed tones, with long pauses to appreciate the sound of the boiling water or the fragrance of the tea.

Cha-no-yu has survived in form if not in meaning. Today, specialized schools thrive by teaching the skills needed to perform the ceremony. It takes at least two years of study to be considered proficient, but the modern version of Cha-no-yu is practiced more as a status symbol than as an aesthetic experience. The overwhelming majority of the tea consumed in Japan today is in the more mundane, less tranquil setting of a factory canteen or crowded restaurant.

Tea in Japan is almost invariably green tea. It is served plain, in small handleless cups. One of the most popular snacks in Japan is *Ocha Zuke,* which is simply a bowl of leftover rice with green tea poured over it.

UBIQUITOUS TEA

Short of an invitation to visit the People's Republic of China, the best way to see how the Chinese take their tea is to visit Taiwan (Formosa).

When you board a train in Taipei, there's a wooden rack with glasses next to each group of seats. Each glass has a fresh supply of tea leaves in the bottom. As the train rolls along, an employee with an enormous kettle travels constantly down the aisle, filling and refilling the glasses. The price of your ticket includes an endless supply of tea, no matter how long the trip.

These same covered glasses are a fixture on every desk, in every business and government office. Take away this fringe benefit and you'd probably have a general strike.

TEA IN THE SKY

The Chinese have always processed tea a special way for trade with Tibet. The tea, which is grown and processed in western Szechuan province, is pressed into bricks that are more easily transported over the high mountain passes. The Tibetans traditionally used this "brick tea" not only to drink, but as a form of currency, each brick having a prescribed value.

The drink itself is more a soup than anything we would recognize as tea. It is boiled, salted, and churned with yak butter, then served in a wooden bowl. Tibetans consume great quantities of this brew, rarely less than fifteen bowls a day, sometimes as many as seventy or eighty.

WILD TEA

In Northern Thailand wild tea, called *miang,* is still gathered in the forests. The mountain people steam and ferment these leaves and mix them with salt and flavorings such as garlic and pork fat. The result is chewed like gum as a stimulant.

PICKLED TEA

In Burma, tea is made into a pickled condiment called *letpet.* To prepare it, fresh tea leaves are boiled until soft. Then they are rolled, cooled, and jammed into a section of bamboo. The bamboo is stoppered with guava leaves and buried until the tea has fermented. This "siloed" tea is mixed with oil, garlic, and dried fish and then eaten as a delicacy.

MOTHER RUSSIA AND HER SAMOVAR

In Russia, tea is usually black. And strong. The traditional form was brick tea, which came in overland caravans from China. Today Russia grows some of her own tea, and imports a great deal more.

The warmth-giving samovar traditionally provided a social focus in Russia's cold climate. The custom was to eat one very heavy meal at midday. The rest of the time the people got by on an almost endless supply of tea.

Tea isn't actually made *in* the samovar. The samovar, usually brass, is a charcoal brazier surrounded by a water chamber that holds up to forty cups of water. The teapot, which rests on top, contains a very concentrated brew of tea. The tea is usually served in glasses, often with metal holders like our old-fashioned soda glasses. A little tea concentrate is poured in the glass, then the glass is filled with water from the samovar. The tea is served with lemon and jam or lump sugar. The jam or sugar may be stirred into the tea, or some may be placed in the mouth first, with the tea sucked over it.

THE MIDDLE EAST

Turkey shares Russia's tradition of tea served from a samovar. Some of the most colorful street merchants in Turkey are the tea vendors. Their elaborate brass tray-tables carry a samovar, tea caddies, lemon, sugar, and glasses to serve the tea.

Since Turkey grows tea, but not coffee, the Turkish government has urged the people to give up their much-loved "Turkish coffee" in favor of the locally produced tea. When I visited Turkey after an absence of fifteen years, I was amazed at how successful this government policy had been in changing a nation's drinking habits.

In Iran, tea is the national drink. Here, and in most of the Arab states, the preference is for green tea.

Green tea is also the favored brew in Morocco, where it is mixed with liberal doses of dried mint and sugar. All serious bargaining is done over a glass of mint tea. When you enter a shop, the owner seems much more concerned with persuading you to accept a glass of tea than he is in giving you information about the merchandise. Too late you realize that having accepted the tea gives the merchant a good ten to fifteen minutes to pitch his wares before you can find any gracious way to exit.

BRITAIN'S "CUPPA"

Tea is so much a part of English life a whole language has grown up around it: the familiar "cuppa," the indispensable "elevensies," "high" and "low" tea. The list could go on and on.

"High" tea, contrary to logic, was the workingman's tea, while "low" tea was of aristocratic origin. Afternoon, or "low" tea, is supposed to have been invented by Anna, the wife of the seventh Duke of Bedford. The aristocracy customarily ate a hearty breakfast. Then, because the servants were off in midday, the family had a light, picnic-style lunch, and a formal dinner at eight or nine o'clock. Anna's innovation was to have the servants bring tea and cakes in the late afternoon, shortly after they returned to work.

"High" tea wasn't to tide you over until dinner — it was in place of it. The working classes usually ate only one substantial meal a day, at lunchtime. After work, the cold meat left from lunch was served along with bread, cheese, and salads as "high" tea.

Afternoon tea in Britain today more closely resembles low tea. And as dinner time has gotten earlier, tea time has moved back to around four o'clock. Of course, four isn't the *only* tea time. "Elevensies" is the late morning tea break. In factories they actually blow a whistle, and everyone queues up at the tea cart.

Chains of tea shops like Lyon's Corner Houses are as popular in England as hamburger stands are in America. In rural areas, it's not unusual to see "TEA" signs in front of private homes, where the family income is supplemented by serving tea to passing travelers.

One aspect of British tea drinking that seems foreign to many Americans is the addition of milk. Addition is probably not the right word. Most Britons put the milk in the cup first, then add the tea. In fact, if you don't want milk in your tea, you'd better say so when you order it.

RULE BRITANNIA

They used to say the sun never set on the British Empire. It finally did, but the British passion for drinking tea seems to have stuck in every country she ever had influence over.

The Irish may hate the English, but they wouldn't be without their cup of tea. North or south, the Irish like their tea good and strong. The name Irish Breakfast refers to just such a hearty blend of black teas, designed so that the flavor will come through even in a cup that's half milk, half tea.

India and Ceylon (now Sri Lanka) were never tea-drinking nations until the British introduced tea cultivation and began promoting tea's consumption. These and all the Commonwealth countries tend to drink tea "in the British fashion," although not necessarily with milk.

In India, every village, no matter how remote, has its tea shop. It may be as simple as a bamboo lean-to with an open fire in a pit in the ground, but the kettle is always on.

The tea shop is the center of social life, and a resting place for travelers. Many have simple rope beds strung in the shade, where a traveler or laborer can nap out of the scorching noonday sun. Unlike the custom in our cafes, where newcomers head for the empty tables, Indians seek the occupied ones. With tea in hand, strangers strike up conversations as if they were old friends.

Even people who are so poor they live in the street and beg for their living start their day with a cup of "chay." Laced with sugar and buffalo milk, it may be the only food they get all day. If a person is too poor to afford even the 2¢ for a cup of tea, someone will buy it for them, or the tea shop will provide it on the house.

In New Zealand and Australia, most tea is consumed in the British manner. The exception is Australia's "Billy Tea," as prepared in the outback. The billy or "Matilda" is a common tin can with a handle to hang it over an open fire. This is the bushman's constant companion, as immortalized in the song "Waltzing Matilda": "And he sang as he watch'd and waited till his billy boil'd/You'll come a waltzing Matilda with me."

The bushman throws a handful of tea leaves into his billy full of water and sets it to boil over the fire. After his morning tea he goes off, leaving the billy simmering. He reheats it in the evening, making a brew you probably have to be a frontiersman to stomach.

Canadians drink considerably more tea than Americans, but they seem to share our love of "convenience foods," including tea bags and instant tea.

In America, tea is rarely served elegantly anymore. Most often what is served is bag tea, or worse, instant. As a social occasion the "tea" still has a place in American life. Receptions and bridal teas are still occasions to bring out the full silver service. I used to go to "tea dances" at the Naval Academy, although I have no memory of tea being served.

When I lived in New York, one of my very favorite ways to spend an afternoon was to have tea in the Palm Court at the Plaza Hotel, complete with string quartet, starched linen, and impeccable service.

And, while the rest of the world may look down its nose at America's custom of drinking iced tea, it certainly has advantages over fatteningly sweet (or chemically sweet) soft drinks.

TEA AND HEALTH

Is tea a boon to health? Or a scourge? There are plenty of *beliefs* about the virtues and vices of tea, but very little proof one way or the other. Unfortunately for those who like to have everything thoroughly documented, tea is so commonplace it seems to be of little interest as a subject of scientific research.

Tea was used in China as a medicine long before it was adopted as a form of refreshment. The Emperor Shen Nung, in the very first written reference to tea, credits it with being:

> . . . good for tumors or abscesses that come about the head, or for ailments of the bladder. It dissipates heat caused by phlegms, or inflammation of the chest. It quenches thirst. It lessens the desire for sleep. It gladdens and cheers the heart.

A fifth century Chinese dictionary states: "The drink renders one sober from intoxication and keeps one awake." The custom of tea drinking and the invention of porcelain are believed to have made possible the enor-

mous growth of China's population. Boiling water for tea kills the potentially hazardous microorganisms in the water. Porcelain's smooth surface can be washed clean so as not to harbor decaying food particles.

When the Japanese Emperor Kammu in 794 A.D. created the position of Supervisor of the Tea Gardens, it was as a position within the Medical Bureau.

The first word to reach Europe concerning tea described it as removing fever, headache, side-pains, aching joints, and even gout. When tea first appeared in Holland, it was sold by apothecaries. It was praised by doctors and laymen alike.

The doctors of Germany and France, however, were critical of tea. In 1635, the German physician Dr. Simon Paulli called tea dangerous to Europeans and claimed that it would hasten death if consumed by people over 40. In France, the entire medical *College de France* attacked China tea and urged the use of local herbs instead.

The first English advertisement for tea, in 1658, describes tea as "That excellent and by all Physicians approved China drink . . . " A hundred years later, Jonas

Hamway attacked tea calling it "pernicious to health, obstructing industry, and impoverishing the neighborhood"; his attack drew a defense from Samuel Johnson. Johnson described himself as a " . . . hardened and shameless tea-drinker, who has for many years diluted his meals with only the infusion of this fascinating plant; whose kettle has scarcely time to cool; who with tea amuses the evening, with tea solaces the midnight, and with tea welcomes the morning."

George III's psychiatrist-jailer, Dr. Willis, suggested that China tea might be the cause of the king's madness. His lack of observation is incredible. Tea by that time was so popular the entire country would have been bulging with lunatics if tea were to blame.

COMMON BELIEFS TODAY

Many of the virtues credited to tea throughout its history are still believed today. And the power of belief being what it is, the fact that many people think tea will make them feel a certain way makes it that much more likely they *will* feel that way when they drink it.

In the middle western states of China, the older generations save their tea leaves after brewing and dry them out to use as stuffing for their pillows. Sleeping on such a pillow is believed to be beneficial to health.

In the West, people who rarely drink tea will put the kettle on at the first sign of a cold. People still use tea to perk themselves up — and to calm themselves down. Many find it settles the stomach, especially after a big meal. Tea is still taken for headaches. And some find it diuretic. What does science say about all this?

TEA AND MODERN SCIENCE

A symposium on the "Pharmacological and Physiologic Effects of Tea" held in 1955 by the New York Academy of Medicine produced the following innocuous definition of tea: "an aqueous infusion of caffein and tannin, a major agricultural crop, a social habit, a nutritional (containing vitamins), dietary (non-caloric) beverage that is almost always medically safe."

Tea's most prominent ingredients, tannin and caffeine, are probably responsible for most of the pros and cons of tea. Caffeine is considered a villain by many, but it also has a number of medically-recognized benefits. The first thing to know is how much caffeine is actually in a cup of tea. Precise measurement is impossible, because of differences in the amount of tea used per cup and the length of time the leaves are allowed to steep. The amount of caffeine is about the same whether the tea is green, black, or Oolong. It is safe to say the amount in an average cup is no more than 1 grain (compared with 3.5 grains in an average cup of coffee).

Caffeine's stimulant properties are widely known, in terms of both mental alertness and physical ability. It is also a frequent ingredient in headache remedies. A 1952 study demonstrated the usefulness of caffeine in treating hypertensive headaches.

Subjectively, the caffeine in tea does not appear to produce undesirable side effects the way it does in coffee ("coffee nerves and insomnia"). One logical explanation for this is that cup-for-cup tea has less than a third as much caffeine as coffee. Another theory is that the *combination* of caffeine and tannin in tea somehow cancels out the negative effects each can have separately.

69

Tannin, which is responsible for tea's flavor, is acidic. By all rights it should irritate the stomach. In fact, most people find tea soothing to the stomach. Why is that? For one thing, free tannin combines with alkaline substances and albumin to form neutral tannates. If milk or cream is added to tea, the tannins combine with the casein, neutralizing the astringency of the tannin. If the tea is drunk straight, the tannins combine with undigested proteins in the stomach. So, either way, the tannins pass through the stomach in a more-or-less neutralized form. In the intestine, the proteins are digested and absorbed, re-releasing the tannin. The mild astringency in the intestine may be slightly constipating. This could be slightly helpful in treating diarrhea.

INCONCLUSIVE RESEARCH

If tea's effects on the body were thoroughly and accurately understood, tea might play an important role in health care. Few substances are cheaper or more readily available. The problem is in establishing indisputable research results. Tea usually is only a small part of a complex diet. A 1941 study noted a low cholesterol level in Chinese subects. Was tea drinking the cause? Or other aspects of diet and lifestyle? Experiments with rabbits showed that tea, taken with or following a meal of fats, prevented a buildup of serum lipids (cholesterol). But rabbits don't ordinarily eat an all-fat diet, and their digestive tract is not the same as a human's. Hopefully, with atherosclerosis such a compelling problem, research will seek to define what role tea might be able to play in controlling this disease. The Tea Research Instiitute of Sri Lanka, in fact, claims to be near to reporting conclusive evidence of tea's ability to reduce cholesterol in the blood.

Another fascinating direction for research is the role of tea in controlling obesity. Obviously, as a non-caloric beverage tea is helpful to dieters. But it might be even more helpful than that. Russian and American studies indicate that tea reduces the enzyme activity of trypsin by half; trypsin is the enzyme that breaks down protein in the digestive system. In a population where overconsumption of protein is more common than protein deficiencies, tea drinking with a heavy protein meal might keep the body from digesting as much of the protein.

For the present, while awaiting science's answers, we'll just have to enjoy our tea and assume it to be, as the symposium concluded, a "beverage that is almost always medically safe."

TEA AS A HOME REMEDY

An unused teabag can be used as a compress to stop external bleeding. This is part of Army first aid training. Some dentists recommend such a compress following a tooth extraction.

A wet tea bag is supposed to extract the sting of a bee bite. It can also be used as a compress for any minor burn. A weak tea solution can also be used as an eye wash. Some consider it especially helpful for red or itchy eyes caused by allergies.

A cold tea bath can be quite soothing for a summer sunburn (because of tea's tannin content). A tea bath can also be used for "tanning" your skin, a neat trick in the winter, when you can't afford a trip to Florida. Simply prepare a batch of iced tea (p.   ), add to your bath water, and soak. Obviously, if you want to tan your face, you'll have to hold your nose and take a total dunking.

The Universal Antidote — of which tea is an integral part — was developed by two Duke University doctors for use when prompt medical attention is not available; it should never be used as a replacement for medical treatment. This is a stop-gap measure, to be used where the nature of the poison is unknown or where no more specific antidote is known.

UNIVERSAL ANTIDOTE

2 parts powdered burnt toast
1 part Milk of Magnesia
1 part strong tea

The burnt toast acts like charcoal, to absorb poisons in the stomach. The Milk of Magnesia helps offset an acid poison, and the tannic acid in the tea helps offset an alkaline poison.

TASSEOMANCY: IS YOUR FUTURE IN THE LEAVES?

During the Middle Ages in Europe, a time when mystical philosophies abounded, all the "black arts" thrived. One of these was divination, or the forecasting of the future. Every sort of commonplace object was used by the seer (mantis) in search of symbols to reveal future events. Aeromancy was a method that involved observation of atmospheric conditions. Alectryomancy used a cock that pecked grain placed on letters of the alphabet. In belomancy, arrows were used. Capromancy looked for symbols in smoke, and so on through the alphabet.

When tea drinking was introduced in Europe, the leaves left in the bottom of the cup logically became a further source of prophetic inspiration, known as tasseomancy. The practice has survived as an amusing pastime, and a featured attraction of "gypsy" tea rooms.

A person with genuine psychic powers may actually be able to see your future in tea leaves. The rest of us will have to content ourselves with the entertainment value of having our leaves read, or learning to read leaves ourselves using the traditional symbolic associations that have been passed down from generation to generation.

The Russian Tea Room, next door to Carnegie Hall in New York, is one of the most famous tea rooms I know of that carries on this tradition. Aside from superb food and tea, it provides a reader, who for a fee will come to your table and tell your fortune from your empty cup. Many cities all over the country have such tea rooms, often called gypsy tea rooms. A visit and a reading are a very pleasurable introduction to the mysteries of this divination. Even if your community lacks such a tea room, don't despair. All you need to stage your own reading is some loose tea, a pot to brew it in, a plain white cup, and a good imagination.

HOW TO READ TEA LEAVES

Loose tea is a must, of course. Tea bags and infusers defeat the whole purpose, which is to end up with leaves in the bottom of your cup. Dump the loose tea in the bottom of a teapot and cover with boiling water, just as you would any time you make tea.

Serve the tea in a cup and saucer. The cup should have a handle and be plain white inside (to eliminate distractions). The handle is important because it represents the subject of the reading and her or his home. It is important for the subject to drink the tea in the cup. Pouring it out is cheating.

When all but a little liquid is gone, the subject holds the tea cup in the left hand and swirls the liquid around three or more times towards their heart. Then the subject turns the cup upside down onto the saucer so the remaining liquid drains out.

After the liquid has had time to drain, the reader picks up the cup and the reading begins. The first omen to look for is a drop of liquid falling from the cup as it is picked up. This indicates tears the subject will experience in the near future. It's not the happiest way to start a reading but it is pretty common and doesn't mean the rest of the reading will be negative.

The reader places the cup in front of her or him, with the handle to the left. The handle represents the direction south. Opposite it, north, nearest the reader, east, and away from the reader, west.

The leaves nearest the rim symbolize events in the immediate future, within a few days. The closer to the bottom of the cup, the more remote the events foretold. A stem or leaf on the rim of the cup symbolizes a man you will meet in the next few days. If another symbol occurs near that one, it may explain in what connection the meeting will occur. For instance, if there is a grouping of leaves shaped like a castle — which symbolizes an unexpected legacy — perhaps the man is a lawyer calling to tell you you're a beneficiary in your late Uncle Charlie's will.

Look at the leaves carefully and use your imagination. Perhaps one grouping looks like a horse, another like a flower. Even specks that don't conjure any images by themselves may line up with other specks to form a straight or wavy line. Notice *where* in the cup these symbols occur. A line that starts near the left side of the handle means a journey. One on the right side of the handle means a visitor. If the line completely circles the cup it means a long journey and return home.

Remember that symbols to the left of the handle are motivated by the subject. To the right of the handle, the action is brought *to* the subject. Also consider the size of the symbols: the larger they are, the more important.

If the cup reveals no patterns, just a mess, it represents a state of confusion or indifference. Just leave it at that. Don't pour a new cup and try again. It is considered bad luck to have a reading more than once a week.

The chart shows some of the traditional symbols and their interpretations in tea leaf reading. Obviously you may see many other objects in the leaves. Use your imagination to ascribe meanings that seem appropriate for that object. That's part of the fun of tea leaf reading. And you are doing this for fun, aren't you?

TEA LEAF SYMBOLS

1. ACORN Success.
2. AIRPLANE Near the handle, do something new. On bottom, a disappointment.
3. ANCHOR Success. If cloudy, means disappointment with loved one.
4. ANGEL Good news.
5. ANTS Difficulties ahead that will mean hard work.
6. APPLE Good health.
7. AXE Obstacles, danger.
8. BABY Near the handle, unexpected honors. On side, financial troubles. On bottom, unhappiness in love.
9. BALL A change is coming.
10. BARREL If full, good luck. If empty, you need rest.
11. BASKET If full, news of a birth. If empty, save your money.
12. BEAR A warning; stay home.
13. BED You need rest.
14. BELL Good news
15. BIRD Good luck.
16. BOAT Proceed with plans.
17. BOOK If open, go ahead with plans. If closed, be cautious.
18. BOTTLE Don't overindulge.
19. BRACELET An important union will take place.
20. BRANCH If leafy, new friend or a birth. If bare, business or social opposition.
21. BRIDGE Your decision will lead to success.
22. BROOM It's time for a change.
23. BUILDING Change your surroundings.
24. BULL Control your temper.
25. BUSH Unexpected money.

26. BUTTERFLY Social pleasures.
27. CAGE Marriage
28. CAR A positive change.
29. CASTLE An unexpected legacy.
30. CAT Beware of false friends.
31. CHAIN Love or marriage.
32. CHAIR An unexpected visitor.
33. CHURCH An invitation to a ceremony.
34. CIRCLE Money.
35. CLOCK Illness.
36. CLOUDS Trouble or doubts.
37. CLOVER Good luck.
38. COFFIN Bad news.
39. COMPASS Travel.
40. COW Prosperity.
41. CROSS Sacrifice.
42. CROWN Success.
43. CUP A new friendship will bring joy.
44. DAGGER Danger.
45. DAISY Love.
46. DEER Be calm.
47. DIAMOND Good luck in love.
48. DOG A trustworthy friend.
49. DONKEY Be patient.
50. DOOR If open, surprising news. If closed, be patient.
51. DOVE Peace, good news.
52. DRAGON Time for a change.
53. DUCK Cheer up.
54. EGG A birth.
55. ELEPHANT Health and happiness.
56. FAN Beware of flirting.

57. FIREPLACE Give a party.
58. FISH Good luck.
59. FLAG A warning.
60. FLIES Don't worry about annoying details.
61. FLOWERS On the side, happiness in love. On the bottom, disappointment in love.
62. FOUNTAIN Prosperity.
63. FOX Deception.
64. FROG Make a change.
65. FRUIT Prosperity.
66. GATE Open, a problem solved. Closed, more negotiations needed.
67. GOAT Don't be stubborn.
68. GRAPES Happiness.
69. GUITAR You need affection.
70. GUN Trouble.
71. HAMMER Eventual success.
72. HAND Friendship.
73. HARP Romance.
74. HAT Money.
75. HEART A lover.
76. HEN Be frugal.
77. HORSE A lover.
78. HORSESHOE Good luck.
79. HOURGLASS Danger.
80. INITIALS People you know or will meet.
81. KETTLE Domestic harmony, unless steaming, which means domestic troubles.
82. KEY Good luck.
83. KITE Don't take chances.
84. KNIFE Beware.

85. LADDER Ambition.
86. LEAVES Hope.
87. LILY Friendship.
88. LINES Parallel lines mean a journey. Straight lines, peacefulness. Wavy or broken lines, uncertainty.
89. MAN You will meet a stranger.
90. MASK Guard your secrets.
91. MOON Honors.
92. MOUNTAINS Hard work ahead.
93. MOUSE Financial troubles.
94. MUSHROOM A lover's quarrel.
95. NUMBER Days, or weeks. May indicate when a nearby symbol will occur.
96. OWL Illness.
97. PIPE Be open-minded.
98. RAT Danger.
99. RING Marriage.
100. SAW Interference.
101. SCISSORS Near the handle, domestic quarrel. Near the rim, a broken marriage. On bottom, trouble at work.
102. SHIP Travel.
103. SNAKE Evil.
104. SPADE Hard work will pay off.
105. SPIDER Unexpected gifts.
106. SQUARE A protection against danger.
107. STAR Health, wealth, and happiness.
108. SWORD Disagreement.
109. TREE Health and prosperity.
110. TRIANGLE Good luck. Upside down, use caution.
111. WHEEL You will be rewarded for hard work.
112. WOMAN A wish will be fulfilled.

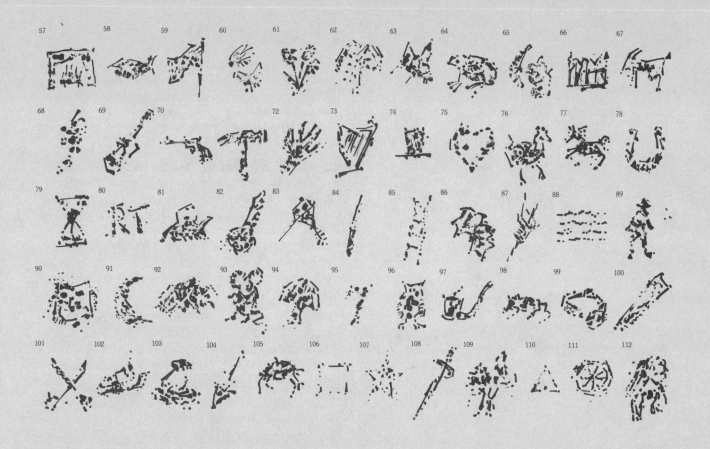

HERBAL TEAS

Herb tea is a catchall name for infusions of an enormous variety of plants. The part of a plant used for making herb tea may be anything from the leaves to the flowers, roots, bark, or seeds. Herb teas can be brewed from fresh or dried ingredients. The tea may consist entirely of one ingredient or a mixture of many.

Originally these infusions (like tea itself) were used as medicine. But many of them have come to be appreciated for their taste as much as for any healthful benefits they may have. Herbal teas are called *Tissanes* in France, where they are far more popular than "China" tea. The same is true in Germany. In Colonial America, herb teas such as "New Jersey Tea" and "Labrador Tea" became popular substitutes when tea was boycotted.

Today we're seeing a renewed interest in herb teas in America. It started with the popularity of health foods. But herb teas are now starting to pop up in a lot of places besides health food stores. You can even buy herb teas in tea bags. Instant herb teas may be next.

Personally, I'm enchanted as much by the lore and the beauty of the plants used in herb teas as I am by the brews themselves. For me, growing or collecting my own ingredients is part of the romance of herb teas.

GATHERING WILD HERBS

No matter where you live there's a good chance wild herbs live there too. Some are native, others originally were domestic plants. Euell Gibbons once found a dozen edible plants growing in a one-block median strip in San Francisco. Herb hunting can be a delightful excuse for an outing. But go about it cautiously; many plants have dangerous look-alikes. Don't use any plant you're not absolutely sure about.

The best way to learn is from someone who knows. More and more community colleges are offering adult education nature courses. These classes often consist of nature walks with a biologist, botanist, or other specialist in the natural sciences. Even if wild herbs aren't the subject of the class, the teacher might be willing (and qualified) to identify herbs. Groups like the Sierra Club or the local natural history museum may also offer classes or guided walks. Next best is a knowledgeable friend. If you know someone who knows wild plants, ask them if they'd be willing to share their knowledge on a nature walk together. More than likely they'll be flattered, and willing.

Books are an enormous, but sometimes confusing, source of information about wild plants. Try to find books specific to your area. Why cart around useless information about marshy plants when you're in the desert? For field identification, you'll need an easy-to-carry, well-illustrated book. Some are illustrated far better than others. Color photographs are best in my opinion. Black and white photographs are sometimes less helpful than good line drawings. See the bibliography for a few suggested books.

If you do go out gathering wild plants, be considerate of the environment and other people. If you want to gather plants on private property, ask the owner's permission. Observe the laws regarding plant collecting on public lands; in many places, it is forbidden. Never take more than you need. And always make sure that what you're taking is plentiful in the area. This is especially true for roots, flowers, and seeds. If you take too much, the plant may disappear from that location forever.

GROWING YOUR OWN

Growing herbs is fun and easy. You don't even need to have a garden. A window sill you can line with pots is space enough. Herbs need sunshine, but usually less care than many other types of plants. The most common herbs, like parsley, sage, and oregano, are usually available as seeds or plants at your local nursery. If you want to try something more exotic, try these mail-order sources:

Sunnybrook Farms Nursery
9448 Mayfield Road
Chesterland, OH 44026.

Herb plants, shipped fresh in 2¼" pots. Twenty-five varieties of thyme alone. Their Bicentennial special is a complete Colonial Herb Garden for $27.50.

Greene Herb Gardens
Greene, RI 02827.

Seeds for dozens of varieties of herbs. Two packets for $1.00, postpaid. Also books.

DRYING HERBS

Herbs can be used fresh, or they can be dried for use later. Drying should be done in a well-ventilated, shady spot. Some people spread them on newspapers. Some hang them in bunches, upside down. Both of those methods have drawbacks. Spread out, the herbs can easily blow away. The ones I've tried to hang seem inclined to fall down as the stems dry out. The best method I've found for drying leafy herbs is in a brown paper bag. Take a large grocery bag and stab it all over with a knife to make ventilation holes. Loosely fill the bag about halfway with the herbs you want to dry. Then crunch the top of the bag together and tie it securely with twine. Hang the bag in a shady spot until the herbs crumble when pinched.

As soon as your herbs are dry (it might take a week or more, depending on the temperature and humidity), strip the leaves from their stems and put the leaves in an opaque or dark-colored glass container with a tight lid. The better your herbs are stored, the better they will hold their fragrance and flavoring potency. Don't plan on putting away more than a year's suppy.

BUYING HERBS AND HERB TEAS

Herb teas are still a treat, even if you don't collect or grow the ingredients. Many herb tea ingredients are also used as cooking spices. Those are easy enough to find in a supermarket. For a bigger selection, try a health food or natural food store. They'll most likely have a good selection of already-blended herb teas as well as the individual ingredients. Coffee and tea specialty stores are also beginning to carry herbs.

Here are two mail-order sources for herbal teas. Both are in the San Francisco Bay area. One offers an extensive selection of individual herbs and herb tea blends. The other specializes in Oriental herb teas, a whole different world to explore.

STAR HERBS
38 Miller Avenue
Mill Valley, CA 94941

A comprehensive catalogue of herbs, spices, herbal teas, and other herbal preparations.

HERB T. CO.
440 Judah Street
San Francisco, CA 94122

A mystifying list of such exotic oriental herb teas as Jyumihaidokuto and (believe it or not) Tokishigyaku-kagoshuyushokyoto. Hopefully they'll soon come out with some descriptive literature to help unravel the mysteries.

MAKING HERB TEAS

Compared with regular tea, herbal tea usually requires more of an herb (or herbs) and a longer steeping time to get a flavorful infusion. I'd suggest two heaping tea-spoonsfuls of dry ingredients per cup of water. If you're using fresh leafy herbs, use twice as much as you would of the dried ingredient. Generally, an herb tea should be steeped five to ten minutes. (Some roots and barks are actually boiled rather than steeped.) There's no one for-mula; your best bet is to get a book that goes into the subject more thoroughly. You'll find some suggestions in the bibliography.

If you'd like to try creating your own herb tea blends, first get acquainted with the individual ingredients. The descriptions that follow may give you some idea of which herbs would appeal to you the most. Once you've selected some, you can buy an ounce of each, brew up individual samples, and make notes on their fragrance and flavor. Then use your intuition to come up with combinations. A number of herbs, especially the cook-ing spices, combine nicely with "real tea." At the end of the descriptions, you'll find some starter recipes for in-spiration.

A BRIEF INTRODUCTION TO SOME FAVORITE HERBS

AGRIMONY

Agrimonia eupatoria The dried leaves and flowers of agrimony (or liverwort) make a tea with a flavor somewhat like apricot. Pliny described it as "good for them that have naughty livers." American Indians supposedly used agrimony to treat fevers. Today, herbalists use it as a digestive aid.

ALFALFA

Medicago sativa Alfalfa is used so widely in the United States as cattle fodder that many people may not be aware of its history as an herb. If you don't find it in an herbal, look again under *Lucerne*. The young leaves and flowers make a bland tea with the fragrance of new-mown hay. Alfalfa is rich in vitamins A, E, D, and K, plus iron and other minerals.

ANGELICA

Angelica archangelica Angelica tea is somewhat bitter, but the fragrance is very much like China tea. With a flavor somewhat like juniper, the herb has long been a popular flavoring for confections and liqueurs such as chartreuse. It is supposedly the "secret" ingredient in some of the aromatic Rhine wines.

ANISE

Pimpinella anisum A favorite cooking spice of ancient Greece and Rome. Anise's strong licorice flavor and aroma make it a popular ingredient in liqueurs. Traditionally considered a digestive aid, the tea is also useful for quieting coughs and breaking up congestion.

BALM

Melissa officinalis Also called lemon balm because of its flavor. It is said that the Welch prince, Llewelyn, who lived to be 108, drank balm tea every morning and evening. Balm tea with lemon and sugar is an old country cold remedy.

BASIL

Ocimum basilicum Native to India, where it is considered sacred to Vishnu and Krishna. An important ingredient in both Italian and French cuisine, basil's flavor and fragrance are somewhat like anise. The fresh leaves are delicious in salads, and form the base of Italian *pesto* sauce.

BAY LAUREL

Laurus nobilis The fragrant leaves of this ancient Mediterranean tree need little introduction. Daphne, pursued by Apollo, was changed into a bay tree. Apollo was the god of poetry, hence the custom of crowning graduates in rhetoric and poetry with a garland of bay leaves, and the title *poet laureate*.

BERGAMOT   *Monarda didyma* Also called Bee Balm and Oswego tea, bergamot is a native North American plant. Oswego tea was popular during the American Revolution as a substitute for the boycotted China tea. The fragrant oil of bergamot is what gives Earl Grey tea its characteristic flavor and fragrance.

BETONY   *Stachys officinalis* Wood betony has a flavor and body somewhat similar to China tea. It is said to be useful in relieving nervous headaches. In some parts of Europe, the dried leaves are smoked as a substitute for tobacco.

BIRCH   *Betula alba* The bark, leaves, and tender twigs of birch make a tea with a flavor similar to wintergreen. Birch is also used in making birch beer and root beer, which are soft drinks. In parts of Europe, the sap is collected and fermented into wine.

BORAGE   *Borrago officinalis* Also called Beebread, the plants are very attractive to bees. The leaves and flowers of borage have a cucumberish flavor and aroma. It has traditionally been added to wine as a flavoring, perhaps the reason for the old proverb: "Borage for courage."

CASSINA   *Ilex cassine* Also called the Christmas Berry Bush, this North American relative of mate was the "black drink" of the Indians of the Carolinas. It was used as a black tea substitute on Southern plantations.

CATNIP   *Nepeta cataria* This aromatic herb, also called catmint, is a member of the mint family, with its characteristic fragrance and flavor. Catnip tea was popular in England long before the arrival of China tea. Catnip tea is a stimulant, and its ability to increase perspiration has made it popular for the treatment of colds and fever.

CHAMOMILE   *Anthemis nobilis* This soft fragrant herb with a hint of the aroma of apples has long been a favorite herb tea in Europe. Its mild sedative effect makes it a perfect after-dinner or bedtime drink.

CINNAMON   *Cinnamomum zeylanicum* One of the world's oldest spices, cinnamon was one of the primary objects of the voyages of the early discoverers. Cinnamon is the peeled inner bark of an evergreen member of the laurel family. It brews into a sweet, pungent tea, and is also a delicious ingredient in spiced black tea.

CLOVES

Eugenia aromatica Cloves began to be imported into Europe as early as the eighth century. In 1265, cloves sold in England for twelve shillings a pound, the equivalent of seventy-two days' wages for a common laborer. The essential oil, oil of cloves, is used in medicines as a carminative and antispasmodic. Pomanders, oranges pierced all over with cloves, were supposed to ward off infection. They are still popular for perfuming clothing. Cloves' antiseptic properties makes it a popular flavoring for toothpaste. The tea is a strong stimulant.

COLTSFOOT

Tussilago farfara This wild herb is a well-established cough remedy. The sweet, strong tea is rich in vitamin C. The dried leaves are often used in herbal tobaccos. It is one of the first plants to bloom in the spring. The flower is similar to a dandelion; the leaves are shaped like a horse's hoof.

COMFREY

Symphytum officinale The common name is a corruption of *con firmare*, from its medieval use to help mend broken bones. The glutinous roots were boiled into a plaster for wounds. A tea made from the dried leaves and ground roots is considered a gentle remedy for diarrhea and dysentery. Its demulcent action has made it popular for treating chest ailments.

DANDELION

Tarraxacum officinale This one shouldn't be hard to find. A slightly bitter tea is made from the leaves and ground roots. It is rich in vitamins and minerals, and the taste can be improved by blending with other herbs. Dandelion wine is made from the flowers. A coffee substitute is made from the ground, roasted roots.

FENNEL

Foeniculum vulgare Similar to anise in both flavor and appearance, fennel grows prolifically as a weed in the San Francisco Bay Area (and elsewhere, I'm sure). The seeds make a refreshing tea. Ancient Chinese and Hindus considered it a remedy for scorpion and snake bites. At one time it was considered a reducing aid. It was also used in various ways to ward off evil spirits. (Stuffing the bedroom keyhole with ground fennel seed was supposed to keep spirits from getting to you in your sleep.)

GINGER

Zingiber officinale Ginger was well known to the Ancient Chinese, and to the Egyptians, who baked a famous gingerbread confection. Elizabeth I set a new fashion by having gingerbread cakes molded in her likeness. While Westerners use ginger mostly in desserts, it is widely used with meats and fish in Oriental cuisine. The tea has a powerful aroma and sweet, peppery taste.

GINSENG

Panax quinquefolium Oriental cultures have, since ancient times, considered the ginseng root a potent and magical herb. Today it is enjoying an incredible surge of popularity in this country, where some people consider it practically a wonder drug. One irony is that Americans pay enormous prices for certain varieties of Korean and other Asian ginseng, while the Chinese value American ginseng above all. The flavor of ginseng tea is quite unique and difficult to describe. You may love it . . . or hate it.

GOLDENROD

Solidago canadensis Called Blue Mountain Tea by the early German settlers in Pennsylvania. At one time, goldenrod tea was exported to China, where it commanded a high price. The fragrant tea has a flavor like anise. It is astringent and diuretic, and is said to help dissolve bladder stones. With goldenrod's reputation as an allergin, hay fever sufferers should perhaps beware.

HIBISCUS

Various Hibiscus species The dried petals of this tropical flower are used in herb tea blends primarily for their coloring, which varies from pink to deep rose. Hibiscus adds a slightly citric taste to a brew.

HOPS

Humulus lupulus The female, cone-like flowers of this vine are the familiar flavoring used since medieval times in brewing beer. Romans ate the young shoots as we do asparagus. Hops tea, made from the leaves and flowers, has a sedative effect and is supposed to improve the appetite.

HOREHOUND

Marrubium vulgare This is one of the five bitter herbs eaten by the Jews during Passover. Horehound candy is a traditional cough remedy. The tea, which has the same musky flavor, is considered good for clearing congestion.

HYSSOP

Hyssopus officinalis The name is from the Greek, *azob* (holy herb), from its use in cleansing holy places. Hyssop tea, brewed from the green tops of the herb, has been used for everything from rheumatism to colds and anemia. Its flavor is bitter and minty.

LABRADOR TEA

Ledum groenlandicum Also called Hudson's Bay Tea and St. James Tea, this was a popular substitute for China tea during the American Revolution and among mountain men and pioneers. The spicy flavor is somewhat reminiscent of China tea.

LAVENDER — *Lavandula spica* A coffee and tea shop near my house sells a tea blend they call Earl Grey that is liberally sprinkled with lavender blossoms. While this may be an unorthodox formulation of Earl Grey, it is a delicious, fragrant drink I highly recommend.

LEMON GRASS — *Andropogon schoenanthus* While this plant is omitted in European herbals, it is a popular seasoning in Indonesian cooking. The tea is mild, and of course lemony. Adds a nice tang when blended with other herbs.

LEMON VERBENA — *Lippia citriodora* Another of the lemon-like herbs, of which there are several. A shrub, which in some cases grows to 15 feet, lemon verbena is a native of Chile and Peru. It is now widely cultivated for its volatile oil.

LINDEN — *Tilia vulgaris* The fragrant dried flowers of this magnificent shade tree make one of the most popular herb teas, especially in France. Linden tea is fragrant and aromatic. It is a household remedy for indigestion and nerves. Honey made from linden flowers is considered the best in the world.

LICORICE — *Glycyrriza glabra* This sweet aromatic root is mentioned as early as the third century B.C. for its value in treating asthma and coughs. In addition to flavoring the ever-popular candy, licorice is widely used in medicines, both for its soothing effect on coughs and for its ability to mask the disagreeable flavor of other medicines.

MARJORAM — *Origanum majorana* This familiar kitchen seasoning was planted on graves by the ancient Greeks to insure the departed's peace and happiness. In the seventeenth century, Gerard described it as "very good against the wambling of the stomacke." The tea is pungent and spicy.

MARSHMALLOW — *Althaea officianlis* The name mallow is from the Greek word for emollient, descriptive of the plant's mucilaginous properties. It is this mucilage that gives marshmallow candy its characteristic texture. For tea, the leaves, roots, and flowers are all used.

MATE   *Ilex Paraguayensis* Also called yerba mate and Paraguay Tea, this South American herb was being used as a tea by the Incas long before the conquistadors arrived. Despite all the coffee in South America, mate is still probably the most popular drink. The leaves (which contain caffeine) are dried and processed like tea. Mate is traditionally infused in a gourd and sipped through a *bombilla*, a straw-like tube with a strainer-bulb at the bottom. The aroma and bitterness may take some getting used to.

MINTS   The three most-used species are *Mentha viridis* (spearmint), *M. Piperita* (peppermint), and *M. Pulegium* (pennyroyal). All make delicious herb teas, alone or with other herbs. In blending, use mint sparingly—it easily dominates more subtle herbs.

NEW JERSEY TEA   *Ceanothus Americanus* This is another of the tea substitutes that grew out of the American Revolution. It produces a tea that in color and taste is similar to green tea.

NUTMEG   *Myristica fragrans* Nutmeg is the dried seed of a tree native to Southeast Asia. The yellow tentacle-like net encasing the seed is mace, which is sold separately, but has much the same flavor and aroma. Freshly grated nutmeg is a pleasure no one should be denied. Try some as tea, alone, or added to black tea.

RASPBERRY   *Rubus strigosus* Tea brewed from raspberry leaves is astringent and stimulating. It has been used as a gargle for cankers and sore throats, and as a soothing drink for children with stomach aches. It is considered especially beneficial during childbirth.

ROSE HIPS   *Rosa canina* While tea may also be made from rose petals, the swelling fruit ("hip") is the most popularly used part of the plant. Rose hips contain an incredible amount of vitamin C, plus other vitamins and minerals. During World War II, rose hips were virtually the only source of vitamin C available in Europe. Rose hip tea is still one of the most popular European herb teas. Its flavor is mellow and acidic. Steep this one a good long time.

ROSEMARY   *Rosemerinus officinalis* Another of the popular seasoning herbs. Because rosemary has traditionally been credited with strengthening the memory, it has come to be the symbol for fidelity between lovers (rosemary for remembrance). It is often used in religious ceremonies, such as weddings and funerals. Tea from the leaves and flowers has a clean, piney taste. It supposedly relieves depression, headaches, and colds.

SAGE

Salvia officinalis The association with wisdom is embedded in its name. Sage was believed to improve the memory and quicken the senses. Sage tea has a strong, camphor-like flavor. It is considered beneficial for relieving nervous headaches and the delirium of fevers, and for improving digestion.

SARSAPARILLA

Smilax officinalis Sarsaparilla was a favorite soft drink of our grandparents' era. Tea made from the ground root has a sharp, licorice flavor. Sarsaparilla was used by the American Indians as a cure for rheumatism and gout. It was introduced to Europe from Mexico as a syphilis cure. (None of these supposed capabilities are medically recognized.)

SASSAFRAS

Sassafras variifolium Another traditional American beverage. Tea is brewed from the bark of the tree's roots. Called "saloop," it used to be sold on London street corners in the early morning. Sassafras tastes much like root beer, of which it is an ingredient.

STAR ANISE

Illicum anisatum Native of southern China. The fragrance and flavor are very similar to *P. anisum*. The name describes the seed pod, which is shaped like a star. As well as being used for tea, star anise is frequently used in Chinese cooking. It is one of the ingredients of soy sauce.

STRAWBERRY

Fragaria vesca Like raspberry, it is the leaves rather than the fruit that are used in brewing strawberry tea. The Indians made tea from the leaves of this native American plant. The tea is mild and fragrant, supposedly helpful in treating diarrhea.

THYME

Thymus vulgaris Thyme is much loved by bees, and thyme honey is considered among the best. Thyme makes a pungent tea with some antiseptic qualities. It is believed to settle the stomach and help induce perspiration.

VALERIAN

Valeriana officinalis During the Middle Ages, this herb was called All-Heal. A tea made from the roots will supposedly induce sleep and ease pain without any narcotic side effects.

WINTERGREEN

Gaultheria procumbens This native American shrub is also called Mountain Tea and Teaberry. The leaves are used both as a tea and to flavor black teas. The tea is stimulating and astringent. It contains methyl salicylate, one of the ingredients in aspirin.

WOODRUFF

Asperula odorata This is the herb that gives German May Wine its characteristic fragrance and taste. The tea is considered by some to resemble the taste of Darjeeling.

HERB TEA RECIPES

MARY'S HERB TEA

Mix together equal parts of peppermint, rose hips, sassafras, anise, and chamomile. To brew one cup, pour boiling water over a heaping teaspoon of the dried herbs, cover, and steep 10 minutes. Serve sweetened with honey.

CASSINA TEA

This is an old Southern recipe from the Carolinas.

In the spring, collect young green leaves from the cassina or Christmas berry bush. Toast in a hot oven, turning constantly, until brown and crumbly. Crush and seal promptly in cans or jars.

To brew, use 1 heaping teaspoon per cup. Add boiling water, cover, and steep all day. Serve in the evening, iced or reheated.

LEMON MINT TEA

For each cup, use 1 t. green tea, one small sprig (or a pinch of dried) spearmint and lemon verbena. Add boiling water, cover, and steep 5 minutes. Strain and serve.

TEA ROSE TEA

For each cup, use 1 t. black tea and 3 or 4 clean, fresh rose petals. Add boiling water, cover, and steep 3 to 4 minutes. Strain and serve sweetened, with one fresh rose petal floating on top.

RECIPES

TEA FOR TEETOTALERS

DRESSED UP TEA

Fine tea, properly brewed, is joy enough in itself. I usually bring it to the table in the teapot, and offer sugar, honey, and milk on the side.

If you want to try something fancier, here are some subtle variations to please the eye as well as the palate:

- Serve hot black tea in a glass cup or mug, topped with a dollop of whipped cream and a dash of cinnamon.

- Float a thin slice of lemon, studded with cloves, in each cup of tea.

- Peel and thinly slice a piece of fresh ginger root. Float a slice in each cup of tea.

- Serve mugs of hot black tea with stir sticks of cinnamon.

- Float a sprig of fresh mint on a cup of hot green tea.

- Instead of sugar, serve a dish of candied orange peel to stir into hot black tea.

ICED TEA-PLUS

Iced tea is always welcome at a picnic, barbecue, or afternoon get-together. These four variations are easy to make ahead for a crowd. Just pour over ice and collect the compliments.

TEA APPLE BLUSH

2 quarts iced tea (black)	4 T. lemon juice
½ C. sugar	¼ t. cinnamon
2 C. apple juice, chilled	¼ t. nutmeg

Make one recipe of iced tea (p. 52). Stir in sugar, cinnamon, and nutmeg and cool to room temperature. Add apple and lemon juice, stir, and serve over ice. Makes about 12 servings.

SPICED ICED TEA

2 quarts iced tea (black)	2 sticks cinnamon
Juice of 6 oranges	1 t. whole cloves
2 C. sugar	

Make one recipe of iced tea (p. 52). Cool. In a saucepan, add 2 quarts of water to the sugar, cinnamon, and cloves and bring to a boil. Strain the syrup and orange juice into the tea. Cool and serve over ice. Makes about 18 servings.

ALOHA ICED TEA

2 quarts iced tea (black)	sugar
1 T. lime juice	fresh pineapple spears
2 C. pineapple juice	

Make one recipe of iced tea (p. 52). When cool, add lime juice, pineapple juice, and sugar to taste. Serve over ice and garnish with spears of fresh pineapple. Makes about 18 servings.

OOLONG COOLER

2 quarts iced tea (Oolong)	2 C. sugar
3 oranges	12 whole cloves
2 lemons	

Make one recipe of iced tea (p. 52). Meanwhile, squeeze the oranges and lemons, saving both the juice and the rinds. In a saucepan, add 2 quarts of water to the sugar, cloves, and lemon and orange rinds. Boil 5 minutes. Remove from heat, add the lemon and orange juice, and strain into the tea. Cool to room temperature and serve over ice. Makes about 18 servings.

SPIRITED TEA

AFTERNOON COOLERS

Don't wait for company to try these delicious coolers. A hot day is excuse enough.

VODKA TEASER

Prepare one recipe of iced tea (p. 52) with any good black tea, but using only 1½ quarts of water. Add a 6 oz. can of frozen orange juice and two 6 oz. cans of frozen lemonade. Cool to room temperature. Add 1 quart vodka. Blend thoroughly and serve over ice.

CHABLIS-TEA FROST

Prepare one recipe of iced tea (p. 52), using green tea and only 1½ quarts of water. Add ¾ C. sugar, stir to dissolve, and cool to room temperature. Add ¾ C. lemon juice and one bottle of chablis. Serve over crushed ice with a mint sprig garnish.

MILD-MANNERED MINT JULEP

As refreshing as its all-bourbon ancestor, with some of the sting removed. Prepare ahead of time a batch of double-strength mint tea or double-strength minted black tea. Let it cool to room temperature. Put the serving glasses (or julep glasses if you're lucky enough to have them) in the freezer for at least half an hour. Finely crush enough ice to fill each glass. In a cocktail shaker or glass, mix for each serving: 1½ oz. of good bourbon, ½ C. of the cooled tea, and simple syrup to taste. When ready to serve, pack the chilled glasses with crushed ice, fill with the tea mixture, and garnish with a sprig of mint. Try to handle the glasses as little as possible to keep the frost on the outside intact. If you've prepared ahead, you'll make a spectacular impression on hot-afternoon callers.

SIMPLE SYRUP

Dissolve equal quantities of sugar and water in a saucepan over medium heat. Pour into a clean, sealable bottle and set aside for sweetening iced tea, coffee, punch, etc. Simple syrup keeps almost indefinitely.

TEA-BASE PUNCHES

Along with alcohol, tea is one of the most popular punch ingredients. Punch doesn't seem to have the popularity today that it once had. But then few people today entertain by the dozens or the hundreds, so it's a little easier to cater individual drinks to the preference of individual guests. In old "receipt" books, it's not unusual to find punch recipes that serve 500 or more. Scaled down, they make a refreshing alternative to the boring "jug of red" or cooler of beer so many people set out for a party today.

GREEN TEA PUNCHES

The older the recipe, the more likely it is to call for green rather than black tea. Here are two examples, one Yankee, one Southern.

PEABODY PUNCH

In 1791, Joseph Peabody of Salem, Massachusetts, retired from the sea to direct his fleet of eighty-three merchant ships and indulge his friends in lavish entertainments. His punch is still a regular at New England parties.

¼ C. green tea	1 quart dark rum
¾ C. sugar	3 C. brandy
Juice of 12 limes	1½ C. madeira
1 C. guava jelly	

Pour 2 cups of boiling water over the tea and steep, covered, for 10 minutes. Strain into a large bowl. Add the sugar and lime juice.

In another bowl, dissolve the guava jelly in 2 cups of boiling water. Add the dissolved jelly to the tea mixture, along with the rum, brandy, and Madeira. Pour into covered jars and refrigerate at least 12 hours.

To serve, pour over a block of ice in a punch bowl. Makes 25 to 30 servings.

CHAMPAGNE PUNCH

This recipe is from the "receipt" book of a Charleston, South Carolina, lady who lived in the 1890s. It conjures in my mind scenes of elegantly gowned ladies and courtly gentlemen strolling on the lawns of some stately plantation.

½ lb. best green tea
12 lbs. sugar
2 cans pineapple chunks
Juice of 5 dozen lemons
1 quart maraschino cherries

10 bottles brandy
10 bottles light rum
12 quarts champagne
12 quarts carbonated water

Five days ahead of time, prepare a syrup with the sugar and 1 quart of water. Boil the syrup until slightly thick, then add the juice from the pineapple and return to a boil. Remove from heat.

Boil 10 quarts of water and pour over tea. Cover and infuse 10 minutes. Strain and cool. Add the syrup, rum, brandy, lemon juice, pineapple, and cherries. Cover and store refrigerated until ready to use. The champagne and carbonated water should also be well chilled. Pour 3 quarts of the liquor-syrup over a block of ice in a large punchbowl. Add a quart each of champagne and carbonated water. Refill in the same proportions as needed. Makes 600 to 650 servings. (Unused liquor-syrup can be saved in tightly corked bottles, in case a few dozen of your guests don't show up.)

BLACK TEA PUNCHES

Black tea contributes color as well as body to a punch. Here's a classic "rum punch" recipe, and an unusual wine one.

RUM PUNCH

I don't know why this is called rum punch, really. There's twice as much brandy in it.

1 quart brandy	1½ T. black tea
1 pint dark rum	Juice of 2 dozen lemons
½ pint peach brandy	3 quarts carbonated water
½ pint Curacao	1½ C. sugar

Pour 1 quart of boiling water over the tea and let steep, covered, for 5 minutes. Strain into a bowl. Dissolve the sugar in the tea, then add the lemon juice and all the liquors. Cover and store refrigerated until ready to use. Pour over ice in a punchbowl. Add carbonated water and garnish with strawberries, cherries, and pineapple chunks. Makes 60 to 70 servings.

RHINE WINE PUNCH

This is a refreshingly different punch, which uses only a little tea.

2 t. black tea	1 pint dry sherry
1 C. sugar	3 bottles Rhine wine
2 C. lemon juice	2 cucumbers
1 C. brandy	1 quart carbonated water

Make a cup of tea, using 2 teaspoons of tea instead of one. Steep, covered, for 5 minutes. Dissolve the sugar in the tea, then add the brandy, sherry, and wine. Peel, seed, and thinly slice the cucumbers. Add to the mixture for 20 minutes, then remove and discard. Pour over a block of ice in a punchbowl and add carbonated water. Makes 30 to 40 servings.

TEA WARMERS

The potential of tea as a hot punch or after-dinner drink has been unjustly overlooked. Here are some suggestions to remedy the oversight.

B 'n B 'n TEA

A very elegant after-dinner drink, especially if served in a glass cup. For each serving, mix 1 ounce of B 'n B liqueur with ½ C. of good hot black tea. Top with whipped cream. Don't stir!

BRANDIED SPICE TEA

Brew a pot or cup of Orange Spice tea (or black tea with cloves and orange peel added to taste). For each serving, add 1 ounce of brandy and 1 teaspoon of honey. Serve hot. Delicious after dinner. Indispensable if you're feeling under the weather with a cold.

WINTER PUNCH

¼ C. black tea	Peel of 1 orange
½ gallon red wine	Peel of 1 lemon
½ C. orange juice	1 C. dark rum
¼ C. lemon juice	1 C. bottled Swedish
1 cinnamon stick	punch

Pour 1 quart of boiling water over the tea leaves and steep, covered, for 5 minutes. Strain the tea into a large pot. Add the wine, lemon and orange juice and peel, and the cinnamon stick. Over medium heat, bring just to a boil. Transfer to a heatproof serving bowl. In a saucepan, heat the rum and Swedish punch. Ignite and pour over the tea mixture. Serve immediately. Makes about 16 servings.

TEA BAVARIAN

Perfect for the holidays, this makes a nice warm change from the usual eggnog. Use the leftover egg whites to make meringues (recipe p. 135).

8 egg yolks	2 t. black tea
Pinch of salt	2 C. rum
½ C. sugar	1 C. milk

Beat the egg yolks and salt in a large bowl until frothy. Add the sugar a tablespoon at a time, beating continuously until the mixture is thick and pale colored.

Pour 1 cup of boiling water over the tea. Cover and steep 5 minutes. Warm the rum and scald the milk in separate saucepans. Beat the strained tea, rum, and milk into the egg mixture. Transfer to a warmed punch bowl and serve immediately. Makes 12 servings.

COOKING WITH TEA

Food recipes that call for tea as one of the ingredients are pretty scarce. It's not surprising that some of the few that do are Oriental. Japanese *Ocha Zuke,* one of Japan's favorite snacks, is simply green tea poured over leftover rice. The two recipes that follow are Chinese — one a simple picnic dish, the other, one of the more elaborate masterpieces of Chinese cuisine.

CHINESE TEA EGGS

Authentically Chinese, these make elegant finger food for a picnic or a party. The color seeps through the cracks in the eggshell, giving the appearance of crazed porcelain.

1 dozen medium eggs	2 T. salt
3 T. black tea	1 T. star anise
3 T. soy sauce	

Hard boil the eggs, then put them in cold water until cool to the touch. Roll the eggs firmly on a smooth surface until they have cracks all around the shell. (DO NOT REMOVE SHELL.) Put cracked eggs and all other ingredients in a saucepan. Add enough water to cover the eggs. Bring to a boil, then reduce heat to a simmer and cook 1 hour. Serve hot or cold, in their shells. They can be stored in the refrigerator for several days in their cooking liquid.

SMOKED TEA DUCK

Next to Peking Duck, this is one of the most prestigious dishes in Chinese cuisine. You'll find it at a few of the most elegant Chinese restaurants. It is very expensive, and often has to be ordered at least a day ahead. You'll understand why when you read the directions. If you're an adventurous cook, don't be put off. Your reward is a dish fit for the Imperial Court.

1 duck, about 4 lb.	2 T. saltpeter
3 T. salt	2 C. wood chips (preferably
2 T. brown (Chinese)	camphorwood)
peppercorn, crushed	½ C. black tea
1 T. grated orange or	1 bunch green onions
lemon peel	1 can sweet bean paste
8 C. peanut oil	

Toast the crushed peppercorns and salt in a dry pan over low heat for 1 minute. Cool, then mix with saltpeter. Rub the duck inside and out with this mixture. Next, make a hook from stout wire and hang the duck over a bowl (to catch any drippings). Dry with an electric fan until very dry (6 hours or more).

Mix the wood chips, tea, and fruit peel thoroughly and place in a large, heavy Dutch oven. Set a clean rock on the mixture, then place the duck on the rock. Cover and smoke over low heat about 10 minutes. Turn the duck and smoke another 5 minutes or until brown.

Place the duck in a steamer and steam 2 hours. (Be sure to check the water level regularly.) Meanwhile, prepare green onions by slicing off roots and green tops so each is 3″ long. (Save the green tops for salad, garnish, etc.) Make 3 or 4 cuts ½″ long into each end of each onion. Put

them in cold water in the refrigerator until ready
to serve. They will open up, or "blossom."

Remove the duck from the steamer and deep fry
in peanut oil until the skin is quite dark and
crispy. Cut into 1" x 2" slices (use a Chinese
cleaver, which cuts through bone and all). Arrange the pieces on a platter and serve accompanied by the green onions and sweet bean
paste. The green onions are traditionally dipped
into the sweet bean paste and eaten in alternate
bites with the duck.

COOKING FOR TEA

TEA SANDWICHES

Tea sandwiches can be delicate or hardy. Although the crusts are traditionally cut off the bread, it's certainly not necessary to do so. All sandwiches are at their best when made with fresh homemade bread. The last two recipes are what I call "whimsy sandwiches," good conversation pieces at a tea or picnic. The gingerbread sandwich is especially popular with children.

PAPRIKA CHICKEN SANDWICHES

1 chicken breast, skinned, boned, & poached	1 t. paprika
8 slices bread	¼ t. cayenne pepper
¼ lb. butter	1 t. lemon juice
1 T. mashed pimiento	Salt & pepper to taste

Soften the butter and mix well with the pimiento, cayenne, lemon juice, and salt and pepper. Trim the crusts from the bread and spread each slice with an equal portion of the butter. Top half the bread with thin slices of chicken. Cover with the remaining slices and cut into triangles or squares.

CURRIED EGG SALAD SANDWICHES

12 slices whole wheat bread	2 t. curry powder
6 hard boiled eggs	1 t. Dijon mustard
2 T. mayonnaise	Salt & pepper to taste
1 T. chutney	

Press the eggs and chutney through a sieve or fine blade of a food mill. Blend in the mayonnaise, mustard, curry powder, and salt and pepper. Trim the crusts from the bread. Spread half the slices with the egg mixture. Top with the remaining slices and cut into quarters.

GUACAMOLE SANDWICHES

1 very ripe avocado
2 T. mayonnaise
1 t. lemon juice
1 T. finely minced onion

½ small tomato, diced
1 clove garlic
Tabasco, salt, & pepper
    to taste

Put peeled and seeded avocado in a small bowl and mash with a fork. Blend in mayonnaise and lemon juice. Squeeze garlic through a garlic press into the mixture. Add tomato and onion and blend thoroughly. Add salt and pepper to taste, plus a dash or more of Tabasco, depending on how hot you want it. Spread on bread and cut into small sandwiches. Cover with close-fitting plastic wrap and refrigerate until served.

DILLED BLUE CUCUMBER SANDWICHES

½ pint sour cream
2 oz. blue cheese, crumbled
1 t. lemon juice

½ t. dill weed
Salt & pepper to taste
½ cucumber, sliced thin

In a small bowl, add crumbled blue cheese to sour cream and blend thoroughly with a fork. Stir in lemon juice, dill weed, and salt and pepper to taste. Cover and chill at least 1 hour. Spread each slice of bread about ¼" thick with this mixture. Cover with a layer of cucumber slices and top with a second slice of bread spread with the blue cheese mixture. Cut into small sandwiches and serve immediately, or refrigerate, covered, until needed.

WATERCRESS SANDWICHES

8 slices bread
¼ lb. butter
2 t. minced fresh
   tarragon, or ½ t. dried
   tarragon

2 t. each, minced fresh
   parsley, chives and
   watercress
8 whole watercress sprigs
1 t. lemon juice
Salt & pepper to taste

Soften the butter and blend well with the herbs, lemon juice, and salt and pepper. Trim the crusts from the bread and spread each slice with an equal amount of the butter. Cover half the slices with 2 watercress sprigs each. Add the top slice to each sandwich and cut each into thirds. Chill, covered, until ready to serve.

GINGERBREAD SANDWICHES

Trim crusts from thinly sliced white bread and cut each slice into 4 squares. For each 2 slices of white bread, cut 1 slice of 1″ thick gingerbread (recipe, p. 133) to fit. Spread both sides of the gingerbread, and 1 side of each slice of white bread with softened cream cheese. Sprinkle with chopped pecans and press the sandwiches gently together.

ROSE PETAL SANDWICHES

Put a ¼ lb. stick of butter in a jar filled with fresh rose petals. Seal and leave in a cool place overnight. The butter will absorb the fragrance and flavor of the petals. Cut the crusts from thinly sliced bread. Cut each slice into four triangles. Spread the triangles with the perfumed butter. On half the slices, arrange some fresh red rose petals, overlapping the edges so they will show in the finished sandwich. Top with the remaining slices and chill, covered, until ready to serve.

FINGER QUICHE

Here's a delicious change of pace from finger sandwiches, for tea, or for hors d'oeuvres. You can make individual quiches in tart pans or the bottom inch of your muffin tins, or make a larger quiche in a pie pan or quiche pan and cut it into bite-size pieces when cool. Serve at room temperature or re-warm in the oven before serving.

Crust

2 C. unbleached white
    flour (or 1 C. each white
    & whole wheat)
½ t. salt

¼ lb. cold butter
3 T. shortening
2 to 5 T. ice water

Sift the flour and salt into a mixing bowl. Flick the butter and shortening into the flour until it is all crumbly with no pieces larger than a pea. Add the least amount of water possible to gather the dough into a ball that can be rolled out. Roll out thin on a floured board. Cut circles to fit your tins for individual quiches. The sides should be about 1" high. Prick the crust several times with a fork. Line the crust with foil, fill with dry beans and bake 10 minutes at 375°. Remove the beans and foil and fill with garnishes and custard.

Garnishes

Grated cheese (Parmesan,
    Swiss, etc.)
Sauteed sliced mushrooms
Diced ham
Crumbled bacon
Spinach, cooked, chopped
    & drained

Canned shrimp, drained
Sauteed onions, sliced
    or diced
Sliced tomatoes
Green peppers, diced

If you're making individual quiches, put different combinations of garnishes in the different wells for a whole variety of flavors. If you're making one large quiche, use one variety of cheese plus any two or three of the other ingredients. It always comes out delicious.

Custard

1 C. whipping cream	4 egg yolks
(or ½ C. whipping cream,	Salt, nutmeg, and cayenne
½ C. half & half)	pepper to taste

Beat the cream, egg yolks, and seasoning until blended. Pour over the garnishes you have sprinkled in the crust, and bake in a 375° oven until puffed and brown (30 to 45 minutes, depending on size). Cool before cutting.

BREADS

CARDAMOM BREAD

This deliciously fragrant white bread is Scandinavian in origin. When my friend Jane Donohue taught me to make it, we devoured the first loaf as soon as it was cool enough to touch. If you're planning to save this one for company, better post a guard at the kitchen door, or bake an extra loaf to throw to the family wolves.

2¼ C. water
½ stick butter
2/3 C. nonfat dry milk
1/3 C. honey

1½ t. ground cardamom
6 C. unbleached flour
2 envelopes yeast
2 eggs

Mix the water, butter, dry milk, sugar, salt, and cardamom in a saucepan. Warm to 120 to 130°. Measure 2¾ C. flour into large bowl. Blend in the yeast, then pour in the warmed liquid and the 2 eggs. Beat for 30 seconds at low speed. Scrape down the bowl, then beat 3 minutes at high speed. Gradually add the remaining flour until the mixture forms a soft dough. Turn the dough onto a floured board and knead until smooth. Put the dough in a greased, covered bowl and let rise until doubled. Punch down and divide the dough into 4 parts. Divide each of these into 3 parts and roll into ropes about 1 ft. to 1½ ft. long. Braid the three ropes together and tuck under the ends. Place the four braided loaves on 2 greased cookie sheets. Cover and let rise on a rack over hot water until doubled in size. Preheat the oven to 375°. Bake 25 to 35 minutes, or until nicely browned. Turn out on a rack to cool.

CORNELL OATMEAL BREAD

I include this recipe because (1) it was developed by my alma mater; (2) it is very nutritious; and (3) it is incredibly delicious with tea (especially toasted).

½ C. warm water
2 envelopes yeast
1/3 C. brown sugar
2 C. uncooked oatmeal
2½ C. boiling water
3 T. oil

4 t. salt
6 C. (or more) unbleached flour
2 T. wheat germ
½ C. soy flour
¾ C. nonfat dry milk

Combine ½ C. warm water with the yeast and brown sugar. Let stand 5 minutes. Combine the oatmeal with the boiling water, oil, and salt. Let it cool. Measure and sift together the flour, wheat germ, soy flour, and dry milk. Stir the yeast mixture into the oatmeal mixture. Add 2½ C. of the flour mixture and beat for 2 minutes. Blend in another 2½ C. of flour mixture and turn onto floured board. Knead for 5 minutes, adding more flour as necessary. Put the dough in a greased, covered bowl and let rise until doubled. Punch down and shape into 2 loaves. Let the loaves rise in a warm, draft-free place until double in size. Preheat the oven to 350° and bake 50 to 60 minutes until the loaves are well browned and have a hollow sound when thumped with a finger.

PEANUT BREAD

2 C. unbleached flour	1 C. dry-roasted peanuts
1 C. sugar	1 C. milk
1 T. baking powder	1 egg
½ t. salt	4 T. butter

Put the peanuts in a blender and grind to a powder. Sift through a sieve into a large bowl. Sift in the flour, sugar, baking powder, and salt. Melt and cool the butter. In another bowl beat together the milk and egg. Blend in the butter, then pour this mixture into the flour mixture and mix thoroughly. Pour the batter into a greased and floured loaf pan and bake in a 350° oven for 50 minutes or until browned and a toothpick inserted in the middle comes out clean. Cool 5 minutes in the pan, then invert on a rack to finish cooling.

SHORTBREADS

Shortbread could (and should) be considered a Scottish national treasure. You'll find tins of imported Scottish shortbread in gourmet shops, but don't hesitate to try making your own. The only "trick" is working with the dough. I finally solved that problem by rolling it out on brown paper and leaving it there through the baking.

Shortbread's ingredients are as plain and simple as can be, but the result is a surprisingly delicious "cookie." It's tempting to gobble them up right from the oven, but do try to make them at least a day ahead of time. Stored in foil or a covered cookie jar, their buttery flavor gets richer and richer with time.

SCOTTISH SHORTBREAD

This authentically Scottish recipe uses a combination of wheat and rice flours. My local health food store grinds the rice flour for me. It adds a nice "tooth" to the shortbread.

¼ lb. butter, softened	1 C. unbleached white flour
1/3 C. sugar	½ C. rice flour
pinch of salt	

Cream together the sugar and softened butter. With your fingers, work in the flour and salt until you can press the dough together into a ball. Divide the dough in half. Form each half into a smooth ball. Cut 2 sheets of brown paper (I use grocery bags) to fit 2 cookie sheets. Press each ball of dough in the center of a cookie sheet and roll into a circle about ½" thick. Score the dough into pie-shaped wedges using the dull edge of a knife. Prick the dough several times with a fork and press lightly all around the edges with the fork (as you would a pie crust). Bake in a 350° oven for 10 minutes. Reduce the heat to 250° and continue baking until lightly browned. Cool on the brown paper, then break into wedges.

OATMEAL SHORTBREAD

Oatmeal is another Scottish favorite. It makes a shortbread that is chewy and delicious.

¼ lb. butter, softened	1 C. unbleached white flour
1/3 C. sugar	2/3 C. uncooked oatmeal
Pinch of salt	

Cream together the sugar and softened butter. Mix the flour, salt, and oatmeal together and work into the butter and sugar with your fingers until you can press the dough together into a ball. Divide the dough in half. Form each half into a ball. Cut 2 sheets of brown paper to fit 2 cookie sheets. Press each ball of dough in the center of a cookie sheet and roll into a circle about ½″ thick. Score the dough into pie-shaped wedges, using the dull edge of a knife. Prick the dough several times with a fork and press lightly all around the edges with the fork (as you would a pie crust). Bake in a 350° oven for 10 minutes. Reduce the heat to 250° and continue baking until lightly browned. Cool on the brown paper, then break into wedges.

SHORTNIN' BREAD

Shortbread with a Southern accent.

¼ lb. butter, softened
¼ C. light brown sugar
Pinch of salt

1½ C. unbleached
white flour

Cream together the butter and brown sugar. With your fingers, work in the flour and salt until you can press the dough together into a ball. Divide the dough in half. Form each half into a smooth ball. Cut 2 sheets of brown paper to fit 2 cookie sheets. Press each ball of dough in the center of a cookie sheet and roll into a circle about ½" thick. Score the dough into pie-shaped wedges, using the dull edge of a knife. Prick the dough several times with a fork and press lightly all around the edges with the fork (as you would a pie crust). Bake in a 350° oven for 10 minutes. Reduce the heat to 250° and continue baking until lightly browned. Cool on the brown paper, then break into wedges.

STRAWBERRY SHORTBREAD TART

When strawberries go out of season, try this delicious cookie-like crust filled with fresh sliced peaches, and so on through the fresh fruit season. As good-looking as it is good-tasting.

Shortbread Crust

1 heaping cup unbleached white flour

3½ T. powdered sugar
½ C. butter, softened

In a mixing bowl, flick all the ingredients together with your fingers until crumbly, with no bits larger than a pea. Press into a pie or tart pan and bake at 350° for 20 minutes. Cool.

Fruit Filling

1 q. strawberries (or other fresh fruit)

1 C. sugar
3 T. cornstarch

Arrange half the strawberies in the cool, baked crust. Put the other half of the berries in a saucepan, add the sugar and cornstarch and mash thoroughly. Bring to a boil, and continue to boil until thick and clear. Cool the mixture, then pour over the strawberries in the crust.

Serve topped with whipped cream flavored with vanilla and sugar.

CRUMPETS

What could be more English than "tea and crumpets"? But what in the heck is a crumpet? Actually, it's almost identical to an English muffin. But baked fresh, a crumpet has a flavor like nothing you ever got from a store. Crumpets are cooked on a greased griddle, using muffin rings (or tuna cans with the lids removed, and well-scrubbed of course).

1 C. hot water
2-2/3 C. scalded milk
2 t. sugar
1 t. salt
1 envelope yeast

2 T. warm water
4 C. unbleached white
  flour
3 T. butter, softened

Combine the first 4 ingredients in a large bowl and cool to room temperature. Dissolve the yeast in the warm water and let stand 10 minutes, then stir into milk mixture. Sift the flour and stir half of it into the milk mixture. Cover the bowl with a damp cloth and set in a warm place to rise for 1½ hours. Beat in the softened butter and the rest of the flour. Let it rise again until doubled.

Butter a griddle and the muffin rings or molds made from cans. Place the rings on the heated griddle and fill each with dough. Cook until the tops are dry and bubbly. Remove the rings and turn the crumpets over to brown the second side. Repeat until all dough is used.

To serve, split and toast the crumpets as you would English muffins. Serve well-buttered and pass the marmalade.

Homemade Marmalade

The best orange marmalade is supposedly that made from Seville oranges, sweet and juicy. This is an authentically British recipe, taken from a well-worn copy of *Mrs. Beeton's Sixpenny Cookery.*

> 12 Seville oranges
> 2 lemons
> Water
> Sugar

Thinly slice the oranges and lemons, peel and all. Remove the seeds and inner pith. Weigh the slices and place in an earthenware crock. Add 3 pints of water for each pound of fruit. Cover and set aside for 3 days.

Pour the fruit into an enameled or stainless steel saucepan and boil gently until tender. Cool the mixture and weigh it again. (If you have first weighed the empty pot, you can weigh the fruit in the pot and just subtract.) Add 1 lb. of sugar for each pound of fruit. Bring to a boil. Skim and cook gently until the syrup stiffens quickly when tested on a cold plate.

Pour into jelly jars and seal with canning lids or paraffin.

TEA SCONES

Next to crumpets, scones are probably the most English thing to serve with tea. Scones are the rich cousin of ordinary biscuits. Not so sweet as cake, they make the perfect in-between for afternoon tea. They're delicious alone or with butter, jam, or honey.

2 C. all-purpose flour
2 T. sugar
1 T. baking powder
1 t. salt

6 T. butter
2 eggs
1/3 C. cream

Sift all the dry ingredients together into a mixing bowl. Blend in the butter with your fingertips or a pastry blender until the mixture is evenly crumbly. Reserve a little of the egg white. Beat the rest of the eggs together with the cream and stir into the dry ingredients. Form the soft dough into a ball and roll out ½" to ¾" thick on a floured board. Cut with a biscuit cutter or into diamond shapes using a sharp knife. Brush the tops with the reserved egg white and bake on an ungreased cookie sheet in a 400° oven for 15 minutes or until lightly browned.

For *Raisin Scones*, add ½ C. raisins to the blended dough.
For *Blueberry Scones*, dust 1 C. fresh blueberries with flour and add to the dry ingredients before adding cream mixture.
For *Cheese Scones*, omit the sugar, and add ½ C. grated sharp cheddar to the blended dough.

CAKES

PRUNE CAKE

¼ lb. butter
1½ C. sugar
3 eggs
2¼ C. flour
1 t. ground cloves
1 t. cinnamon

¼ t. salt
¾ C. buttermilk
1½ t. baking soda
1½ C. chopped cooked
   prunes
1 C. chopped walnuts

Cream together the sugar and softened butter. Add the eggs one at a time, beating well after each. Sift the flour together with the cloves, cinnamon, and salt. Stir the baking soda into the buttermilk. Add the flour mixture and the buttermilk mixture alternately to the egg mixture. Stir in the chopped prunes and walnuts, making sure they are evenly distributed. Pour the batter into a greased and floured cake pan and bake in a 350° oven for 30 minutes, or until a toothpick inserted in the middle comes out clean. Cool in the pan for 10 minutes, then invert onto a rack to finish cooling. Frost the top with *Cream 'n Cream Frosting* and cut into squares.

Cream 'n Cream Frosting

8 oz. pkg. cream cheese
½ C. milk
3 T. honey

1 t. grated lemon rind
½ C. whipping cream
2 T. powdered sugar

Mix the softened cream cheese with the milk, honey, and lemon rind. In another bowl, whip the cream, sifting the powdered sugar into it. Fold into the cheese mixture and spread evenly over the cake.

APPLESAUCE CAKE

When I moved into a house with a Gravenstein apple tree in the back yard, I started making applesauce to use up my yardful of apples. Then I started hunting out recipes to use up my closetful of applesauce. This is a nice moist spice cake, good for snacking, great with tea.

1 C. shortening
1 C. sugar
2 eggs
1 C. applesauce
1 t. soda
2 C. unbleached flour

1 t. cinnamon
½ t. nutmeg
½ t. ground cloves
1 C. currants
1 C. raisins

Cream the sugar and shortening together with an electric mixer. Add the eggs and continue to beat until smooth. Stir the soda into the applesauce, then add to the mixing bowl. Sift the cinnamon, nutmeg, and cloves with the flour, and add gradually, continuing to beat at medium speed. Stir in the currants and raisins (or use 2 C. raisins). Pour the batter into a greased square or loaf pan and bake in a 350° oven for 40 minutes.

FRUITCAKE FIT FOR A QUEEN

While thumbing through a battered old copy of *Mrs. Beeton's Sixpenny Cookery* I came across a clipping from the July 5, 1958, *Saturday Evening Post*. The scrap of paper read: "For afternoon tea, the Queen likes nothing so much as a rich fruitcake. Frequently I made her Dundee Cake . . ." I don't know which queen — Elizabeth presumably. At any rate, here's the recipe:

DUNDEE CAKE

½ lb. margarine (butter)
⅛ lb. lard (shortening)
½ lb. brown sugar
3 eggs
¾ lb. self-raising flour

¼ lb. ground almonds
¾ lb. sultanas (raisins)
½ lb. currants
¼ lb. candied orange peel
Rind & juice of 1 lemon

Mix the fats, sugar, and grated lemon rind together. Beat in the eggs one at a time. Add the lemon juice. Mix the flour and almonds together and blend in gradually. Stir in the fruit. Spoon into a greased loaf pan and bake 30 minutes at 400°. Lower the heat to 275° and continue baking 1¼ hours.

CREAM CHEESE POUND CAKE

I'm not opposed to using convenience products if the results are this delicious. Truly the best poundcake I've ever tasted. Dieters beware!

3 C. Bisquick
½ C. unbleached white flour
1½ C. granulated sugar
1½ sticks butter, room temperature

8 oz. cream cheese, room temperature
6 eggs
1 t. vanilla
½ t. salt

Cream butter and sugar in a large mixing bowl. Blend in cream cheese and eggs, one at a time. Blend in the Bisquick, flour, salt, and vanilla and beat at medium speed 4 minutes.

Pour into greased and sugared loaf, angel food, or bundt pan and bake at 350° for one hour. Invert on cake rack to cool. When cooled, sprinkle with powdered sugar.

VARIATIONS:

(1) Brown sugar instead of white.
(2) Lemon flavoring and grated lemon rind instead of vanilla.
(3) Add ½ to 1 C. chopped pecans or walnuts.

BEST-OF-THEM-ALL CARROT CAKE

Of the dozens of carrot cake recipes around, this one stands head and shoulders above the rest.

2 C. flour
1½ t. baking soda
1 t. baking powder
2 t. cinnamon
½ t. salt
2 C. sugar
1¼ C. peanut oil

4 eggs
½ C. crushed pineapple & juice
1 C. chopped pecans or walnuts
2 C. finely grated carrots

Sift together the first 5 ingredients. In a large mixing bowl, blend together the sugar, oil, and eggs. Add the dry ingredients and blend thoroughly. Add the remaining ingredients and blend for 5 minutes. Pour into a greased loaf, angel food, or bundt pan and bake at 350° for 40 minutes. Invert on a cake rack to cool.

Orange Glaze

1 C. sugar
¼ C. cornstarch
1 C. freshly squeezed orange juice

1 t. lemon juice
2 T. butter
2 T. grated orange peel
¼ t. salt

Blend the sugar and cornstarch together in a saucepan. Add the orange and lemon juice, blending well. Add the butter, orange peel, and salt and cook over low heat until thick and shiny. Cool completely before glazing cake.

APPLE UPSIDE-DOWN GINGERBREAD

Gingerbread is one of our most ancient sweets, going back at least to the Romans. But upside-down cakes are a product of early American ingenuity, a way to "bake" a cake without an oven. Traditionally prepared in an iron skillet on top of the stove, they are equally delicious cooked in a cake pan in the oven.

¾ C. butter
½ C. granulated sugar
1 egg
1 C. dark molasses
2½ C. flour
1½ t. soda
1 t. cinnamon

1 t. ginger
½ t. ground cloves
½ t. salt
1 C. hot water
½ C. firmly packed
   brown sugar
1½ C. sliced fresh or
   canned apples

In a large mixing bowl, cream together ½ C. butter and the granulated sugar. Add the egg and beat 1 minute. Blend in the molasses. Sift together the flour, soda, and seasonings. Blend gradually into the first mixture. Add hot water and continue blending until smooth.

Melt the remaining ¼ C. of butter and pour into a large iron skillet or 9" × 13" pan. Sprinkle the brown sugar over the butter and arrange the apple slices evenly around the pan. Pour the batter over and bake at 325° for 35 minutes or until a toothpick inserted in the center comes out clean. Invert on serving plate and cool. Serve garnished with whipped cream.

FUNNEL CAKES

This traditional Pennsylvania Dutch specialty is usually served with syrup or molasses. With this slightly sweeter batter and no syrup, they make delicious finger food to serve with tea.

1 egg
2/3 C. milk
1¼ C. unbleached flour
¼ C. granulated sugar
1 t. baking soda

¾ t. baking powder
¼ t. salt
½ t. cinnamon
Vegetable oil
Powdered sugar

Sift together all dry ingredients except powdered sugar. Beat together the egg and milk. Add the dry ingredients and beat until smooth.

Pour oil 2" deep in a 12" skillet. Heat to 375°. Hold your finger over the end of a funnel with a ½" opening. Pour ¼ C. of batter into the funnel. Drip the batter into a circular pattern in the hot oil, starting at the center. Cook until lightly browned, about 2 minutes on each side. Remove to paper towels to drain. Keep the funnel cakes warm while you make up the remaining batter. When they are all done, sprinkle with powdered sugar and serve immediately.

I seem to have any number of recipes that leave me with surplus egg whites. If you do too, I recommend using them up in either of these delicious tea sweets:

MERINGUES

The secret of a successful meringue is a slow, slow oven. The meringues shouldn't brown at all during the long drying-out. If your lowest oven setting still isn't low enough, try opening the door a crack.

Individual meringues are delicious filled with whipped cream and fresh fruit such as strawberries. Or filled with ice cream topped with hot fudge sauce. If you have a pastry bag and tips, the meringue can be piped into lovely decorative shapes.

4 egg whites	⅛ t. cream of tartar
1 t. vanilla	1 C. powdered sugar, sifted

When the egg whites reach room temperature, whip with an electric mixer or egg beater until foamy. Add the vanilla and cream of tartar, and while continuing to whip, add the sugar a tablespoon at a time. Continue to whip until egg whites form stiff peaks.

Cut brown paper to fit two cookie sheets. Place six large spoonfuls on each sheet. With a spoon, make a depression in the center of each. Place in a 225° oven for an hour or more, until thoroughly dry. Turn off the oven, open the door, and leave meringues inside for another 5 minutes. Then cool on their paper and peel off to serve.

WALNUT CRUNCH BARS

1 lb. walnut meats,
  finely chopped
1 C. granulated sugar

1 t. lemon juice
4 egg whites
¾ C. powdered sugar

Toss the walnuts and sugar together. Add the lemon juice and 3 egg whites. Knead the mixture until it sticks together. Pat out ½" thick on a sugared board. Whip the remaining egg until foamy. Continue whipping, adding a tablespoon of powdered sugar at a time until mixture is stiff. Spread over the walnut mixture and cut into ¾" × 1½" bars. Arrange on well-greased cookie sheet and bake at 200° for 20 minutes.

LEMON BARS

This recipe, given to me by my friend Rebecca Archey, is one of the all-time, best-ever things you can put in your mouth. I have yet to serve it to anyone who didn't ask for the recipe.

    1 C. flour
    ½ C. butter
    ¼ C. powdered sugar

Crumble together until the butter is the size of a small pea. Press gently into a 9″ square pan and bake at 350° for 20 minutes. While this is baking, prepare the following:

2 eggs
1 C. sugar
1/3 C. lemon juice

Dash salt
2 T. flour
1 t. baking powder

Mix together the first 4 ingredients, then fold in the flour/baking powder mixture. When the "crust" comes out of the oven, pour this mixture over it and return to the oven for another 25 minutes. Remove from the oven, sift powdered sugar over the top, and let cool before cutting into squares.

DATE NUT BARS

3 eggs
1 C. sugar
1 scant cup unbleached
    flour
1 t. baking powder
Pinch of salt
¼ t. cloves

¼ t. cinnamon
½ t. allspice
1 t. vanilla
2 C. pitted, chopped
    dates
1 C. chopped pecans
Confectioner's sugar

Beat the eggs until light. Add the sugar a little at a time, blending until light. Sift together the flour, baking powder, salt, and spices. Add a little at a time to the egg mixture until thoroughly blended. Add the vanilla and the chopped dates and pecans.

Pour the batter into a greased and sugared 9″ × 13″ pan and bake at 325° for 25 minutes. Cool, cut into 1″ × 2½″ bars, and dust with sifted confectioner's sugar.

BIBLIOGRAPHY

Clair, Colin. *of Herbs & Spices*. New York: Abelard-Schuman Ltd., 1961.

Fitzgerald, C. P. *The Horizon History of China*. New York: American Heritage Publishing Co., Inc., 1969.

Gibson, Walter B. and Litzka R. *The Complete Illustrated Book of Divination and Prophecy*. Garden City, New York: Doubleday & Co., Inc., 1973.

Grieve, Mrs. M. *A Modern Herbal*. 2 vols. New York: Dover Publications, Inc., 1971.

Huxley, Gervas. *Talking of Tea*. Ivyland, Pa.: John Wagner & Sons Inc., 1956.

Leek, Sybil. *The Sybil Leek Book of Fortune Telling*. New York: Macmillan, 1969.

Lust, John. *The Herb Book*. New York: Bantam Books, 1974.

Schapira, Joel, David, and Karl. *The Book of Coffee & Tea*. New York: St. Martin's Press, 1975.

Shalleck, Jamie. *Tea*. New York: The Viking Press, 1972.

Ukers, William H. *All About Tea*. 2 vols. New York: The Tea & Coffee Trade Journal Company, 1935.

RECIPE INDEX